Governance of Indian State Power Utilities

DIRECTIONS IN DEVELOPMENT
Energy and Mining

Governance of Indian State Power Utilities
An Ongoing Journey

Sheoli Pargal and Kristy Mayer

© 2014 International Bank for Reconstruction and Development / The World Bank
1818 H Street NW, Washington, DC 20433
Telephone: 202-473-1000; Internet: www.worldbank.org

Some rights reserved

1 2 3 4   17 16 15 14

This work is a product of the staff of The World Bank with external contributions. The findings, interpretations, and conclusions expressed in this work do not necessarily reflect the views of The World Bank, its Board of Executive Directors, or the governments they represent. The World Bank does not guarantee the accuracy of the data included in this work. The boundaries, colors, denominations, and other information shown on any map in this work do not imply any judgment on the part of The World Bank concerning the legal status of any territory or the endorsement or acceptance of such boundaries.
   Nothing herein shall constitute or be considered to be a limitation upon or waiver of the privileges and immunities of The World Bank, all of which are specifically reserved.

Rights and Permissions

This work is available under the Creative Commons Attribution 3.0 IGO license (CC BY 3.0 IGO) http://creativecommons.org/licenses/by/3.0/igo. Under the Creative Commons Attribution license, you are free to copy, distribute, transmit, and adapt this work, including for commercial purposes, under the following conditions:

Attribution—Please cite the work as follows: Pargal, Sheoli, and Kristy Mayer. 2014. *Governance of Indian State Power Utilities: An Ongoing Journey*. Directions in Development. Washington, DC: World Bank. doi:10.1596/978-1-4648-0303-1. License: Creative Commons Attribution CC BY 3.0 IGO.

Translations—If you create a translation of this work, please add the following disclaimer along with the attribution: *This translation was not created by The World Bank and should not be considered an official World Bank translation. The World Bank shall not be liable for any content or error in this translation.*

Adaptations—If you create an adaptation of this work, please add the following disclaimer along with the attribution: *This is an adaptation of an original work by The World Bank. Views and opinions expressed in the adaptation are the sole responsibility of the author or authors of the adaptation and are not endorsed by The World Bank.*

Third-party content—The World Bank does not necessarily own each component of the content contained within the work. The World Bank therefore does not warrant that the use of any third-party-owned individual component or part contained in the work will not infringe on the rights of those third parties. The risk of claims resulting from such infringement rests solely with you. If you wish to re-use a component of the work, it is your responsibility to determine whether permission is needed for that re-use and to obtain permission from the copyright owner. Examples of components can include, but are not limited to, tables, figures, or images.

All queries on rights and licenses should be addressed to the Publishing and Knowledge Division, The World Bank, 1818 H Street NW, Washington, DC 20433, USA; fax: 202-522-2625; e-mail: pubrights@worldbank.org.

ISBN (paper): 978-1-4648-0303-1
ISBN (electronic): 978-1-4648-0304-8
DOI: 10.1596/978-1-4648-0303-1

Cover photo: NOAA. This photograph is in the public domain and available for public use. Please credit NOAA.

Library of Congress Cataloging-in-Publication data has been requested.

Contents

Acknowledgments	*ix*
About the Authors	*xi*
Executive Summary	*xiii*
Abbreviations	*xvii*

Chapter 1	**Introduction**	1
	Notes	3
	References	4
Chapter 2	**Institutional Context**	5
	Notes	7
	References	7
Chapter 3	**Corporate Governance of State Power Utilities**	9
	Objectives of Unbundling and Corporatizing State Utilities	11
	Corporate Governance Requirements for State Utilities in India	13
	Findings—Corporate Governance in Practice	14
	Notes	34
	References	36
Chapter 4	**Regulatory Governance**	39
	Mandates of SERCs	40
	Implementation of Regulatory Mandates	41
	Institutional Design: SERC Autonomy, Capacity, Transparency, and Accountability	52
	Indexes on Institutional Design and Implementation of Mandates	59
	Notes	64
	References	66
Chapter 5	**Relationships between Governance and Utility Performance**	67
	Corporate Governance	69

	Governance and Performance	74
	Notes	78
Chapter 6	**Conclusions**	**79**
	Corporate Governance	79
	Regulatory Governance	80
	Recommendations	82
	Notes	85
	References	85
Appendix A	Corporate Governance Requirements in India	87
	Notes	89
	Reference	89
Appendix B	Coverage of Electricity Utilities	91
Appendix C	Utility Performance on Corporate Governance Indexes	95
Appendix D	Corporate Governance Data	97
Appendix E	Coverage of State Electricity Regulatory Commissions	103
Appendix F	SERC Performance on Regulatory Governance Indexes	105
Appendix G	Regulatory Governance Data	107

Boxes

3.1	Literature on Corporate Governance	10
3.2	Types of Directors	14
3.3	Shunglu Committee Recommendations on Corporate and Regulatory Governance	15
3.4	Corporate Governance as an Instrument of Change in West Bengal	29
3.5	Corporate Governance in a High Performing Joint Venture—Tata Power (Delhi)	31
3.6	Organizational Transformation and a Turnaround in Performance in Gujarat	31
4.1	SERC Responsibilities	42
4.2	The Cost of Regulatory Assets	46
4.3	Involving Consumers as Stakeholders: Selected SERC Experiences	58
6.1	MoUs	84

Figures

2.1	Timeline—Establishment of SERCs	6
2.2	Timeline of Power Sector Unbundling (Orange) and Central Electricity Acts and Policies (Green)	6
3.1	Power Sector Structures, 2010	12
3.2	Utilities with More than Two Government Directors	17
3.3	Government Involvement in Different Utility Decisions	18
3.4	Utilities with Board Share of Independent Directors Meeting DPE Guidelines	19
3.5	Utilities That Have a Dedicated Regulatory Cell	20
3.6	Utilities That File Their Accounts on Time and Make Accounts and Audit Reports Public	21
3.7	Average Chairperson/Managing Director Tenure	22
3.8	Number of Directors on Utility Boards	23
3.9	Average Number of Board Meetings per Year	24
3.10	Utilities with Audit Committees	25
3.11	Utilities with an Independent Director Chairing the Audit Committee	25
3.12	Utilities with Executive Directors Constituting Less or More than Half of Board Members	26
3.13	Utilities with an ERP System or Advanced MIS	26
4.1	Ratio of Average Billed Tariff to Operating-Cost-Recovery Level and to Average Operating Cost, 2010	43
4.2	Change in Ratio of Average Billed Tariff to Operating-Cost-Recovery Level, 2003–10	44
4.3	Measures Taken by SERCs to Protect Consumer Rights	48
4.4	Number of Regulations Notified by SERCs	49
4.5	Types of Regulations Notified by SERCs	50
4.6	Action Taken on OA by SERCs	51
4.7	Action Taken on Renewable Energy and Energy Efficiency by SERCs	52
4.8	Share of SERC Budget from Own Resources	53
4.9	Tenure of Chairperson and Other Commission Members	54
4.10	SERC Budget per Household	55
4.11	SERC Staff Strength	56
4.12	SERC Activities Related to Participation and Transparency	57
4.13	Index of Institutional Design vs. Index of Implementation of Mandates	61
4.14	Institutional Design Index Scores	62
4.15	Implementation of Mandates Index Scores	62
5.1	Detailed CG Index Score vs. Profit per Unit Excluding Subsidies	71
5.2	Institutional Design Index and Implementation of Mandates Index vs. Profit per Unit Including Subsidies	73

Tables

3.1	Share of Utilities in Compliance with Indicators That Constitute the Basic Index	28
3.2	Characteristics of the Top Five Utilities Covered in the Detailed Index	29
3.3	Utility Performance on the Detailed Index	33
3.4	Correlation among Corporate Governance (CG) Variables	34
4.1	Indexes of SERC Institutional Design and Implementation of Regulatory Mandates	60
4.2	Correlation among Components of Institutional Design Index	63
4.3	Correlation among Components of Implementation of Mandates Index	63
5.1	Summary Statistics	68
5.2	Correlation between Corporate Governance Variables and Performance	70
5.3	Correlation between Regulatory Governance Indexes and Utility Performance	72
5.4	Regression of Utility Performance on State, Utility, and Corporate Governance Variables, 2010	75
5.5	Regression of Utility Performance on State, Utility, and Corporate Governance Variables, 2011	76
5.6	Regression of Utility Performance on State, Utility, and Regulatory Governance Variables, 2010	77
5.7	Regression of Utility Performance on State, Utility, and Regulatory Governance Variables, 2011	77
B.1	Coverage of Electricity Utilities	92
C.1	Basic and Detailed Index Scores	95
D.1	Basic Corporate Governance Data	98
D.2	Detailed Corporate Governance Data	101
E.1	Coverage of SERCs	104
F.1	Regulatory Governance Index Scores	106
G.1	Institutional Design Data	108
G.2	Implementation of Mandates Data: Tariffs and Standards of Performance	109
G.3	Implementation of Mandates Data: Consumer Protection and Other Regulations	110
G.4	Implementation of Mandates Data: Open Access and Renewable Energy/Energy Efficiency	111

Acknowledgments

This review was carried out by the World Bank at the request of the Department of Economic Affairs of the Ministry of Finance in India under the auspices of the umbrella work program titled India Power Sector Review, led by Sheoli Pargal and Sudeshna Ghosh Banerjee.

The report relies on background research and data collected by a consulting team from PricewaterhouseCoopers, India, led by Ashok Varma and Debasis Mohapatra and supplemented by information provided by a consulting team from Deloitte, India, led by Shubhranshu Patnaik and Anujesh Dwivedi. Amrita Kundu, Pranav Vaidya, and Joeri de Wit provided critical quality assurance. Ian Driscall, Rohit Mittal, Sudeshna Ghosh Banerjee, Mohua Mukherjee, Mani Khurana, Kavita Saraswat, Praveer Sinha, Luis Alberto Andres, Sebastian Azumendi, and Ashish Khanna provided essential constructive inputs. The authors thank Prabhat Mishra and Ashish Vachhani from the Department of Economic Affairs of the Ministry of Finance for useful conversations while framing the review, and the members of the Technical Advisory Panel for the India Power Sector Review, especially J. L. Bajaj, Shantanu Dixit, and Sunil Mitra, for advice and suggestions throughout. Finally, the authors thank the peer reviewers, Alex Berg and John Nellis, for substantive, helpful comments.

Financial support from the Energy Sector Management Assistance Program is gratefully acknowledged.

Bruce Ross-Larson, Jonathan Aspin, and Jack Harlow at Communications Development Incorporated edited this report.

About the Authors

Sheoli Pargal is an economic adviser in the World Bank's Department for Sustainable Development in the South Asia region. She has worked across infrastructure sectors on a range of topics including regulation and governance, private sector participation, public-private partnerships, and industrial pollution, with a focus on analytical and technical advisory work. In 20 years at the World Bank she has had assignments in the research department; the Latin America and Caribbean, Europe and Central Asia, and South Asia regions; and corporate policy and operations units. She has also worked in the Planning Commission in India. Pargal has a PhD in economics from Northwestern University and BA and MA degrees in economics from St. Stephen's College and the Delhi School of Economics, respectively, at Delhi University.

Kristy Mayer is a quantitative analyst with Opower, Arlington, VA. Most recently she was an energy economist in the World Bank's Department for Sustainable Development in the South Asia region, where she focused on electricity tariffs and subsidies, electricity sector regulation, electricity system financial modeling, and energy efficiency. She has also worked at the Federal Reserve Bank of New York and at the U.S. Department of the Treasury. Mayer has an MPA in economic policy from Princeton University and a BA in economics from New York University.

Executive Summary

By the late 1990s, the technical and financial performance of the power sector in India had deteriorated to the point where the Government of India had to step in to bail out the state utilities, almost all of which were vertically integrated state electricity boards (SEBs). Considering that the dismal performance of state utilities reflected internal and external shortfalls in governance, the new Electricity Act of 2003 (EA 2003) mandated the unbundling and corporatization of the SEBs, along with the establishment of independent regulators. This was expected to bring about a more accountable and commercial performance culture, with concomitant results in improved utility performance.

Ten years after the passage of the act, this review looks at the quality of both corporate and regulatory governance in the power sector. It assesses aspects of corporate governance that would be expected to increase internal and external accountability of utilities and so improve their performance. It reviews the institutional design of state-level regulation and assesses the extent to which regulators have implemented key elements of their mandate, since both would be expected to impact utility performance. Finally, this review examines the correlations between the adoption of recommended corporate governance practices and utility performance (indicated by profit) and between regulatory governance (including the institutional structure and functioning of the regulator) and utility performance.

The analysis draws on utility- and state-level data gathered under the India Power Sector Review. The data for this review are quantitative and qualitative information on aspects of corporate and regulatory governance as of 2010 that were collected from interviews, utility and state electricity regulatory commission (SERC) annual reports, and annual account statements.[1] The data cover 69 utilities in 19 states and all 28 SERCs. This report also draws upon financial and operational data from the Power Finance Corporation's Reports on the Performance of State Power Utilities for selected years. In addition, gross domestic product data from the Reserve Bank of India were compiled for each state.

This review finds that the initiatives taken by the government on both corporate and regulatory governance are steps in the right direction. A handful of utilities and state regulators are at the forefront of recommended practices, but implementation varies considerably across the country. For the majority of utilities and states, governance clearly has a long way to go, especially if it is to bring about a more accountable, commercially oriented culture in the sector and improve the efficiency of service delivery and overall financial and operational sustainability.

Corporate Governance

The main finding of this review is that, while most state-level power utilities are substantially in compliance with the basic corporate governance requirements of the Companies Act (that they are mandated to follow), significantly fewer follow the more demanding guidelines issued by the Department of Public Enterprises (DPE) that apply to centrally owned enterprises and are recommended for state-owned enterprises. For example, though almost all utilities have an audit committee, only 28 percent have an independent director heading the audit committee, and only 56 percent have any other specialized board committees. Utilities tend to have more government and executive directors than recommended and fewer independent directors; in fact, only 14 percent of utilities have the recommended percentage of independent directors on their boards and many lack independent directors entirely. Tenure of the chairperson/managing director was an average of only 2.24 years (as opposed to the recommended appointment of 3–5 years) in the utilities reviewed.

Boards remain state-dominated, lack sufficient decision-making authority in practice, and are rarely evaluated on performance. Political interference in appointments to and by the board and in decision making on business aspects remains common, and board member training and peer evaluation are conspicuous by their absence. Professionalizing and empowering boards is a key agenda item for the future.

Finally, few utilities have put the necessary processes and systems in place to support their boards. Less than half the utilities have an advanced management information system that would provide real-time information to the management and board, and no utility has a corporate performance monitoring system. Only about one-quarter of utilities consider merit when making promotion decisions, and only half have a well-defined employee training policy. These aspects suggest that organizational transformation is still a work in progress.

The empirical analysis shows that going beyond the Companies Act and implementing the governance practices recommended by the DPE is associated with higher utility profit per unit. An increase in the percentage of independent directors on corporate utility boards and a decrease in the percentage of executive directors are both associated with better financial performance. In addition, the utilities that have developed information-driven processes, created sound mechanisms for performance management, and made their accounts and audits publicly available are the top performers. Thus the potential rewards of organizational transformation in terms of improved performance outcomes are very attractive.

Regulatory Governance

SERCs have been established in all states, though some as late as 2011. They are expected to prevent political interference in the sector and protect the interests of different stakeholders by regulating utility operations and tariffs. However, they face an enormous challenge in that almost all the utilities they regulate are state-owned. This can limit the effectiveness of standard regulatory mechanisms, which need to be adapted to the incentive structure of public enterprises.

Key responsibilities of SERCs are that they issue licenses for distribution and intrastate transmission; ensure nondiscriminatory open access to both transmission and distribution systems to promote competition and support the development of a multibuyer market and power trading; regulate and rationalize tariffs so as to cover costs; implement multiyear tariff frameworks to reduce uncertainty and encourage investment in the sector; establish and monitor standards with respect to quality and reliability of service by licensees; and safeguard consumer interests, including by setting up mechanisms to redress grievances. In addition, SERCs are tasked with drafting, notifying, and implementing a range of other regulations.

The ability of SERCs to carry out their mandates depends on the technical, financial, and human resources available to them, their competence, their autonomy in decision making (including insulation from political pressures), and, finally, their accountability, all of which fall under the rubric of institutional design. The analysis carried out in this review shows that there is a significant positive association between these features and profit per unit, which underlines how important a robust regulatory framework is for utility operations.

However, this review finds that most SERCs are still some way from an institutional design that would permit them to effectively implement their mandates. Most important, there is no clear accountability mechanism to govern SERCs themselves. In addition, SERCs have generally struggled to achieve true autonomy from state governments, in part because of relationships built into the EA 2003 itself. Many SERCs also lack the resources that might help them perform their functions—most notably, enough professional staff and appropriate information technology systems. Finally, most SERCs have yet to adopt adequate transparency measures and create frameworks for meaningful public input to the regulatory process, although a few have institutionalized "best practice" mechanisms for participatory decision making.

This review also examined SERCs' implementation of their mandates, covering six key areas identified in the governing legislation: tariffs, standards of performance, protection of consumer rights, open access, renewable energy, and regulation in other areas. Most SERCs have yet to fully implement the mandates given them in the EA 2003. While tariffs cover average cost in a majority of states, very few states issue multiyear tariffs. Most SERCs are nominally complying with mandates to promote consumer empowerment and to increase transparency to the public, but need to do far more to ensure that consumers are given opportunities to engage with them and that high-quality information is available to the public. Also, though most SERCs have notified[2] the key regulations necessary to enact the mandates of the EA 2003, many SERCs have yet to take concrete steps to actually implement these regulations. The review finds that the key dimensions of institutional design described earlier are significantly positively correlated with implementation of regulatory mandates.

Recommendations

The agendas on corporate and regulatory governance need further development and are of urgent importance. Establishing an arm's-length relationship between the state and the regulator and between the state and the utility, as intended by reforms initiated even before the EA 2003, is still a priority for the sector.

The empirical analysis underlines the potential benefits from professionalizing and empowering utility boards, bringing in more independent directors, and, in general, implementing corporate governance good practices (for example, the guidelines issued by the DPE) more fully. One potential mechanism would be to incentivize utilities to comply with requirements for listing ("shadow" listing), which could straight away bring greater autonomy and accountability to the boards of state utilities.

In parallel, all dimensions of the institutional design of regulation (autonomy, transparency, capacity, and accountability) need to be enhanced. In the absence of active and interested state legislatures (to which SERCs are technically accountable), other ideas for increasing regulatory accountability should be explored. Potential options include extending the mandate of the Appellate Tribunal to encompass regular monitoring of regulators, monitoring by peers in the Forum of Regulators with full public disclosure of findings, and periodic evaluation by the Planning Commission.

Notes

1. PricewaterhouseCoopers collected the corporate governance and most of the regulatory governance data. Their data were supplemented by regulatory governance data collected from SERC annual reports by Deloitte.
2. In India, "notifying" a regulation means the regulation has been published in the necessary channels and is enforceable.

Abbreviations

ABT	availability-based tariff
ARR	annual revenue requirement
AT&C	aggregate technical and commercial
CG	corporate governance
CGRF	consumer grievance-redressal forum
CMD	chairman and managing director
CPSE	central public sector enterprise
CPSU	central public sector undertaking
discom	distribution company
DPE	Department of Public Enterprises
DSM	demand-side management
EA 2003	Electricity Act of 2003
ERP	enterprise resource planning
FIT	feed-in-tariff
GDP	gross domestic product
genco	generation company
IAS	Indian Administrative Service
ID	institutional design
IM	implementation of mandates
IT	information technology
MIS	management information system
MoU	memorandum of understanding
MYT	multiyear tariff
OA	open access
PAT	profit after tax
RIMS	Regulatory Information Management System
RPO	renewable purchase obligation
SAC	state advisory committee
SEB	state electricity board
SEBI	Securities and Exchange Board of India

SERC	state electricity regulatory commission
SOE	state-owned enterprise
SoP	standards of performance
ToD	time-of-day
transco	transmission company

CHAPTER 1

Introduction

The reform of the Indian power sector initiated in the 1990s was largely motivated by the need to improve the financial performance of the vertically integrated state electricity boards (SEBs) that had come into being with the Electricity Supply Act of 1948. A combination of political interference and weak accountability over the years meant that state-owned utilities had come to have little incentive to perform well, leading to large and increasing commercial losses.[1]

While subject to commercial accounting rules from 1985, SEBs were not companies under the law and were run by their respective state governments through "executive instructions" that "eliminated autonomy, accountability and innovation by SEB employees" and provided no inducement to maximize efficiency and effectiveness (Ruet 2001). Expert opinion was that commercialization and competition were critical challenges for the sector and that limiting state government control (exercised without accountability) over SEBs would be crucial in improving their performance:

> The core of reform is better governance. State governments have controlled their SEBs closely through key appointments, tariff setting, investment approvals and financing, employment conditions, and bureaucratic processes. Initiatives to improve governance must address both sector governance and corporate governance—only thus can the states create an environment in which investors and operators face reasonable commercial risks and consumers, regulators, and other stakeholders honor the contractual rights of utilities to recover their revenues (Besant-Jones 2002).

In line with this thinking, the Electricity Act of 2003 (EA 2003) mandated both the establishment of independent state electricity regulatory commissions (SERCs) and the unbundling of SEBs, with the successor entities coming under the purview of the Companies Act of 1956.[2] Structural change was considered a prerequisite for strengthening utility governance and moving the sector toward operating on commercial principles. Unbundling SEBs into separate business units responsible for generation, transmission, and distribution would make transparent the contribution of each entity to overall performance, and bringing them all under the purview of the Companies Act would require the preparation and independent audit of utility accounts, both of which could be expected to increase accountability; corporatization would insulate them from political interference.[3] Establishing regulators that were independent of the government was considered critical to the creation of a transparent and unbiased governance framework for the sector that could balance consumer and investor and utility interests.[4]

Taking this history as its starting point, this review presents the findings of an empirical examination of utility- and state-level corporate and regulatory governance practices in the Indian power sector. It also attempts to identify whether better corporate and regulatory governance is associated with stronger financial and operational performance of utilities. A key contribution of the review is the collection and presentation of data on key measures of corporate and sector governance for a large sample of utilities and for all states in the country. In addition, this is one of the first attempts to systematically explore the relationship between governance structures and utility-level performance outcomes by exploiting interstate and interutility variations across India.

To bring utilities to a more commercial orientation and thus achieve efficient service delivery, efforts need not only to focus on strengthening the utility's management and internal operations—people, systems, and processes (Ruet 2001)—but also on improving the governance framework and institutional environment in which the utility operates. The utility will, after all, have to respond to external stakeholders such as government (as owner), consumers, regulators, and lenders.

Utilities are subject to two main sets of accountability relationships: accountability to external stakeholders, which is conditioned by the institutional environment in which the utility operates; and internal accountability for results, which looks at how management and staff are held accountable for effectiveness and efficiency. Key indicators of external accountability include whether the utility is subject to well-defined performance targets, uses external auditors, can secure financing from external sources on its own credentials, and is subject to an independent regulator—and whether external groups are represented on the utility's advisory or oversight bodies. Indicators of internal accountability include the responsiveness of the chief executive to the board; whether performance targets are well defined and provide incentives, sanctions, or both; whether staff are subject to annual performance evaluations; whether they have incentives for achieving performance targets; and whether staff receive training to perform their jobs (Baietti, Kingdom, and von Ginnekin 2006).

While ownership, corporate oversight, and service provision are not necessarily separated in public utilities that are organized as a ministry or department, they are generally separated in state-owned companies, in accordance with company law. As public corporations, a board of directors is appointed for the utility, executive management is placed in charge of day-to-day operations, and the accounts are separated from those of other state organizations (Baietti, Kingdom, and von Ginnekin 2006). Well-run public utilities tend to be insulated from political interference, exhibit managerial autonomy (notably over personnel, investment, and procurement decisions), have a degree of financial autonomy in that they generate revenues that at least cover operating costs, and are accountable and responsive to key stakeholders.

This analysis draws on utility- and state-level data gathered under the India Power Sector Review. The data for this review are quantitative and qualitative information on aspects of corporate and regulatory governance and on the functioning and management of utilities and state regulators as of 2010. The data were collected in interviews, and from utility and SERC annual reports and annual account statements.[5] The data cover 69 utilities in 19 states and all 28 SERCs. The report also draws on financial and operational data from the Power Finance Corporation's Reports on Performance of State Power Utilities for selected years. In addition, gross domestic product (GDP) data from the Reserve Bank of India were compiled for each state.

The rest of this review is organized as follows. Chapter 2 summarizes the institutional context and relevant developments over the past two decades. Chapter 3 focuses on the corporate governance agenda adopted by the government and its implementation, specifically relating to the structure and functioning of utility boards of directors. Chapter 4 reviews SERC regulatory governance. Chapter 5 analyzes the correlation between key indicators of the quality of regulatory and corporate governance and utility financial performance. And chapter 6 concludes.

Notes

1. See Report of the Shunglu Committee 2011 (annex 10); Prayas Energy Group 2003; Ruet (2001): "As far back as 1996 the Government of India was concerned about poor management in SEBs and political interference in the day-to-day affairs of the board. Not only were investment decisions not subject to financial evaluation, but the state government interfered in recruitment, promotion, and transfers and undermined efforts to limit theft of power"; Bhatia and Gulati (2004): "In India, electricity theft leads to annual losses estimated at US$4.5 billion, about 1.5 percent of GDP. … What stops governments from eliminating electricity theft? Vested interests of such stakeholders as politicians, bureaucrats, labor unions, utility employees, and consumers. Because of political interference and weak accountability, state-owned utilities have little incentive to improve their performance."
2. EA 2003, Part X, Part XIII. As is evident from the content of the EA 2003, the Government of India's incentives were quite different from the incentives of state governments.
3. Ruet 2003. The promoters of reform also argued for unbundling or de-integration of the former SEBs into generation, transmission, and distribution companies: "The aim was to assess the results and responsibilities among the various activities by de-integration." Also, Vete n.d.: "The Electricity Act of 2003 envisaged the "functional disaggregation of generation, transmission, and distribution with a view to creating independent profit centers and accountability."
4. As countries have moved away from the traditional public sector model and introduced private participation in infrastructure, it has become important to establish

credible regulatory frameworks—including regulatory rules and institutions—to protect the interests of consumers but also those of the public and private parties to infrastructure arrangements. See, for example, Bertolini (2004).

5. PricewaterhouseCoopers collected the corporate governance and most of the regulatory governance data. Their data were supplemented by regulatory governance data collected from SERC annual reports by Deloitte.

References

Baietti, Aldo, William Kingdom, and Meike von Ginnekin. 2006. "Characteristics of Well Performing Public Water Utilities." Water and Sanitation Supply Working Note 9, World Bank, Washington, DC.

Bertolini, Lorenzo. 2004. "Regulating Utilities: Contracting Out Regulatory Functions." Public Policy for the Private Sector Note 269, World Bank, Washington, DC.

Besant-Jones, John. 2002. "Power for India: Strategy for Reform of State Level Power Distribution." Unpublished manuscript.

Bhatia, Bhavana, and Mohinder Gulati. 2004. "Reforming the Power Sector: Controlling Electricity Theft and Improving Revenue." Public Policy for the Private Sector Note 272, World Bank, Washington, DC.

Prayas Energy Group. 2003. "A Good Beginning but Challenges Galore: A Survey Based Study of Resources, Transparency, and Public Participation in Electricity Regulatory Commissions in India." Prayas Occasional Report –1/2003. Pune, India.

Ruet, Joël. 2001. "Winners and Losers of the SEB Reforms: An Organizational Analysis." French Research Institutes in India, 1.

———. 2003. "The Entreprisation of the State Electricity Boards." In *Against the Current: Organizational Restructuring of State Electricity Boards*, edited by Joël Ruet. New Delhi: CSH-Manohar Publishers.

Shunglu Committee. 2011. *Report of High-Level Panel on Financial Position of Distribution Utilities*. New Delhi: Planning Commission, Government of India.

Vete, Anay. n.d. "Review of the Electricity Act 2003." Working Paper 11, Department of Economics, University of Mumbai.

CHAPTER 2

Institutional Context

Over the past two decades, the Indian power sector has moved decisively toward independent regulation of unbundled and corporatized utilities in a process largely led by the states. Orissa led the way by creating an electricity regulator and unbundling—and not just corporatizing but actually privatizing—its distribution utilities (figure 2.1). The Orissa Electricity Reform Act was passed in 1995; the Orissa Electricity Regulatory Commission was established in 1996, at which point the state government initiated the unbundling of the Orissa state electricity board (SEB). Several states followed.[1] Partly in recognition of the need for a consistent approach across the country, the Electricity Regulatory Commission Act was passed in 1998. This Act established the Central Electricity Regulatory Commission and provided the legal basis for creating independent state electricity regulatory commissions (SERCs), which had a mandate to set electricity tariffs, monitor the quality of service, adjudicate disputes, and redress grievances in their states (Tongia 2003).

The Electricity Act of 2003 (EA 2003), which replaced the Electricity Regulatory Commission Act, gave regulators a central role in supporting competition in the power sector, regulating tariffs, promoting open access to the network infrastructure, and specifying standards for quality of service. In addition, the EA 2003 mandated that states unbundle and corporatize their electricity utilities.

As of 2011, all the states and Delhi had created electricity regulators (some jointly with other states—Manipur with Mizoram and Goa jointly with the Union Territories). Of the 29 states (including Delhi) in India, 18 have unbundled their power sectors—some as early as 1996 (Orissa) and others only as recently as 2010 (Meghalaya, Tamil Nadu, Himachal Pradesh, and Punjab) (figure 2.2).[2] Eight of the states that unbundled their SEBs have a holding company, of which the unbundled utilities are subsidiaries (see figure 3.1). All but three states have fully unbundled the generation, transmission, and distribution functions,[3] and nine states have more than one distribution company. The remaining 11 states have yet to unbundle their power sectors, and most still have state-run SEBs or power departments. The one exception is Tripura, which has corporatized its utility (as in the unbundled states) but kept it as a bundled entity.

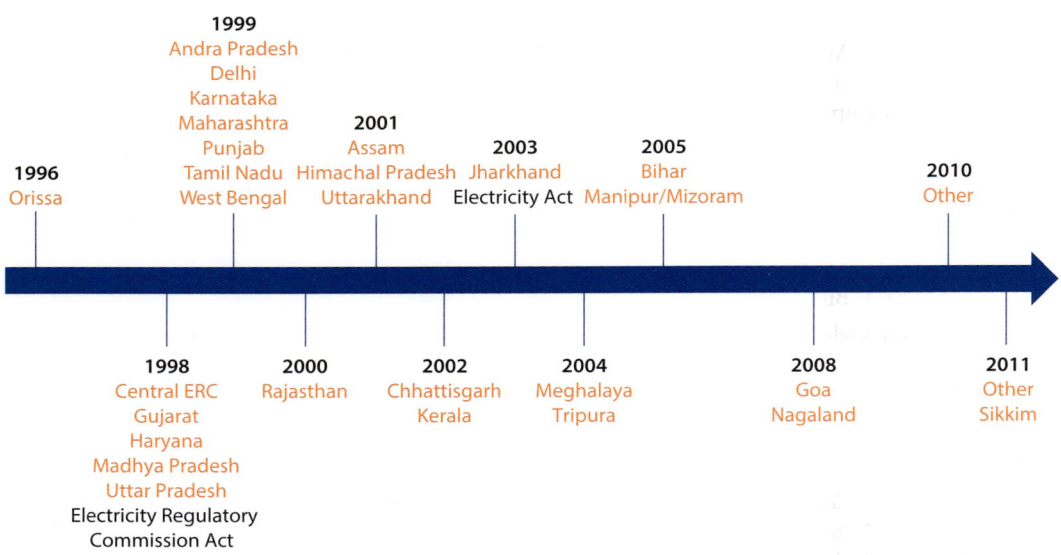

Figure 2.1 Timeline—Establishment of SERCs

Source: World Bank compilation.
Note: ERC = electricity regulatory commission; SERC = state electricity regulatory commission. Indian states are in orange; policy is in black.

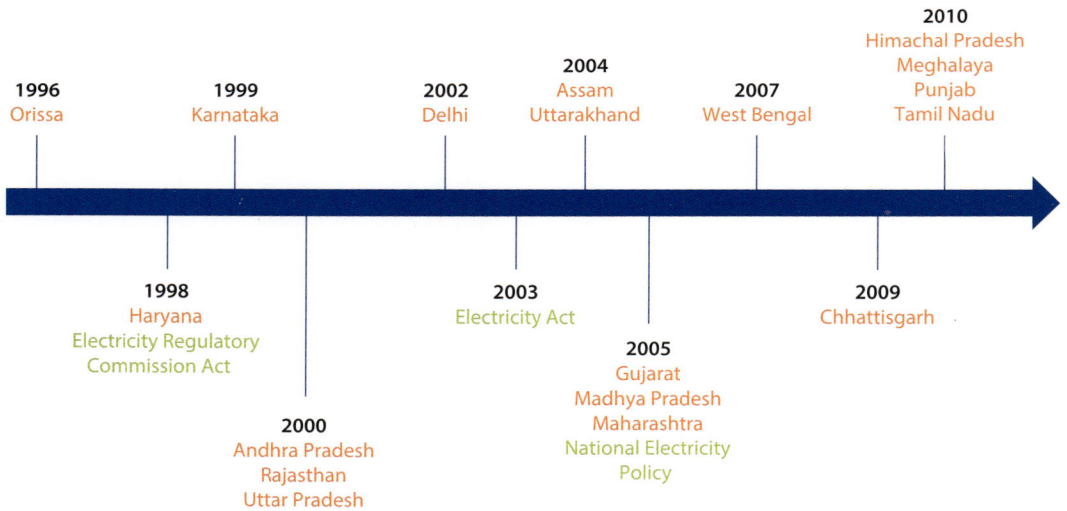

Figure 2.2 Timeline of Power Sector Unbundling (Orange) and Central Electricity Acts and Policies (Green)

Source: World Bank compilation.

Notes

1. Haryana was next with its Electricity Reform Act in 1997 and the establishment of its SERC in 1998. Andhra Pradesh, Karnataka, Uttar Pradesh, Madhya Pradesh, Delhi, and Rajasthan also passed their own state Electricity Reform Acts, which paved the way for setting up SERCs and subsequently unbundling their SEBs. See Dubash and Rajan (2002) and Prayas Energy Group (2003).
2. Bihar in fact unbundled in November 2012 and now has a holding company with four subsidiaries—Bihar State Power Generation Company Ltd., North Bihar Power Distribution Company Ltd., South Bihar Power Distribution Company Ltd., and Bihar State Power Transmission Company Ltd.—but as this review uses data from 2010 and 2011, Bihar is included as bundled.
3. Punjab, Tamil Nadu, and Himachal Pradesh still have a combined generation company and distribution company.

References

Dubash, Navroz K., and Sudhir Rajan. 2002. "India: Electricity Reform under Political Constraints." In *Power Politics: Equity and Environment in Electricity Reform*, edited by Navroz K. Dubash, 51–74. Washington, DC: World Resources Institute.

Prayas Energy Group. 2003. "A Good Beginning but Challenges Galore: A Survey Based Study of Resources, Transparency, and Public Participation in Electricity Regulatory Commissions in India." Prayas Occasional Report –1/2003. Pune, India.

Tongia, Rahul. 2003. "The Political Economy of Indian Power Sector Reforms." Working Paper, Program on Energy and Sustainable Development, Stanford University, Stanford, CA.

CHAPTER 3

Corporate Governance of State Power Utilities

Corporate governance (CG) is "the system by which companies are directed and controlled" (Cadbury Committee 1992). More broadly, it deals with mechanisms by which stakeholders of a corporation exercise control over corporate insiders and management such that their interests are protected (John and Senbet 1997). It specifies the rights, responsibilities, and accountabilities of the different stakeholders in a corporation (namely, the board, management, and shareholders) and key attributes of the processes for corporate decision making. In doing so, it defines a structure for setting a company's objectives, the means for attaining those objectives, and a framework for monitoring performance.[1]

The rise of equity shareholding and the need to protect the rights of investors and equity owners has led to a renewed focus on the quality of board oversight, role of auditors, accountability of management, and transparency of decision making in recent years. Particularly following well-publicized cases of corporate malfeasance in the United States in the late 1990s and early 2000s, there has been greater attention to the quality of CG and independent oversight of firms and renewed efforts internationally, as well as in India, to strengthen the framework regulating their operations.[2]

Indian power sector utilities at state level are insulated from some of the accountability pressures that firms are generally subject to from equity owners and even creditors. Most are publicly owned, with ownership vested in the state (rather than central) government, and unlisted, so not subject to the discipline of stock markets. At the same time, being utilities, their operational performance is shaped by the framework of tariffs, performance standards, and the like established by regulators. Public ownership, moreover, means that the interests of owners may differ from the typical objectives of profit maximization or maximizing shareholder value over time associated with a private corporation. In state-owned enterprises (SOEs), the financial objective is typically one of sustainability, and it may be coupled with distributional equity and other public policy objectives that conflict with the financial objective, since the set of stakeholders is broadened to include employees, consumers, suppliers, and the government. Thus SOEs can be subject to the whims of a shifting group of stakeholders that may not prioritize financial performance or may not even have a public-good objective. In a public utility, therefore, the board has to ensure not only that managerial and staff incentives are aligned with the utility's public policy goals but also that the utility is sufficiently insulated from political pressures.

Stylized results from the empirical literature on CG point to the importance of board size and composition, as measured by the "insider-outsider" ratio (directors associated with the firm vs. independent directors), in affecting company performance. Other key indicators of CG considered likely to affect entity performance include turnover or tenure and stability of the CEO; quality of board members (having robust processes for board selection and evaluation); board access to information and hence the quality of its discussions; and the extent to which it is insulated from government interference. Box 3.1 summarizes findings from the literature on CG practices, notably in SOEs.

Box 3.1 Literature on Corporate Governance

A significant body of work exists on corporate governance (CG) and boards of directors, primarily investigating the effect of board composition, structure, and behavior on the role the board performs and the effect on firm performance. Several papers provide comprehensive surveys of different aspects of the CG literature. John and Senbet (1997) survey the empirical and theoretical literature on CG mechanisms with a focus on internal mechanisms (such as boards of directors) and their role in ameliorating firms' agency problems. Fields and Keys (2003) review the empirical research on the role outside directors play in monitoring managers; the impact of board diversity; incentives for corporate executives to manage firm earnings; and managerial incentives to bear risk. They find that an independent, diverse board is associated with better performance, reduced earnings management, and reduced risk-taking activity by management.

Hermalin and Weisbach (2003) survey the economic literature on boards, looking at board composition, board size, specific board tasks (CEO hiring and firing, executive compensation), and factors that affect boards' makeup. They find that board composition is not related to performance, while board size is negatively related to it. Composition and size appear related to the quality of the board's decisions on CEO replacement, acquisitions, "poison pills," and executive compensation. Adams, Hermalin, and Weisbach (2009) survey the literature with an emphasis on research done after the Hermalin and Weisbach survey. They find that the two most commonly asked questions are: What determines boards' makeup? And what determines their actions?

Wong (2004) and Vagliasindi (2008) both focus on state-owned enterprises (SOEs). They identify the key differences between SOEs and private-sector firms and make recommendations to improve the governance of SOEs and bring their governance closer to that of the

box continues next page

Box 3.1 Literature on Corporate Governance *(continued)*

private sector. They include recommendations for how the government should conduct itself as the SOE owner and recommendations for structuring SOE boards to improve performance and increase accountability. In its 2005 *OECD Guidelines on Corporate Governance of State-owned Enterprises,* the OECD proposes similar recommendations to those made by Wong and Vagliasindi. The recommendations are generally similar to India's CG guidelines as well.

A few studies have focused on the impact of CG in India. Black and Khanna (2007) and Fagernas (2006) report on the impact of the CG regulations issued by the Securities and Exchange Board of India (SEBI). Black and Khanna find that firms covered by SEBI experienced larger stock price gains than other firms in the days following the announcement of the new regulations, while Fagernas finds that the introduction of the regulations was associated with an increased tendency for firms to explicitly tie CEO pay to the firm's performance. Ghosh (2006) finds a negative association between board size and firm performance and a small, positive association between firm performance and the number of nonexecutive directors.

Objectives of Unbundling and Corporatizing State Utilities

Unbundling State Electricity Boards (SEBs) to create distinct corporate bodies (companies) with independent accounts and staff was expected to lead to greater transparency in the operational performance of each element in the service delivery chain, in turn creating incentives for each element to achieve a profit (Tongia 2003). Corporatization itself was intended to create an arm's-length relationship between the state government and the utility, thus creating space for commercial operation of the latter.

Despite being unbundled, it is relatively common for the unbundled utilities to remain under a single holding company with powers delegated to the holding company (figure 3.1). It is questionable whether such unbundled companies are actually run as distinct entities, as the chairperson of the board of the holding company and of the boards of the successor companies is often the same person and, indeed, there may be partial or full overlap in board membership. In many cases, this structure thus undermines the main reason for unbundling and obfuscates the lines of accountability.[3] The system is also potentially expensive because it creates an additional layer between the government (owner) and the companies—though it may insulate companies from government interference.

Establishing holding companies—initially an interim measure to handle staff pension liabilities—has been used to address staff concerns about their pensions once they are assigned to a successor company. However, inherited staff and human resource policies requiring staff to be absorbed by the successor companies restrict companies' freedom to manage themselves as commercial entities. Perhaps as a result, only half of the states that unbundled their SEBs have finalized staff transfer and created separate cadres for each of the unbundled entities.

Figure 3.1 Power Sector Structures, 2010

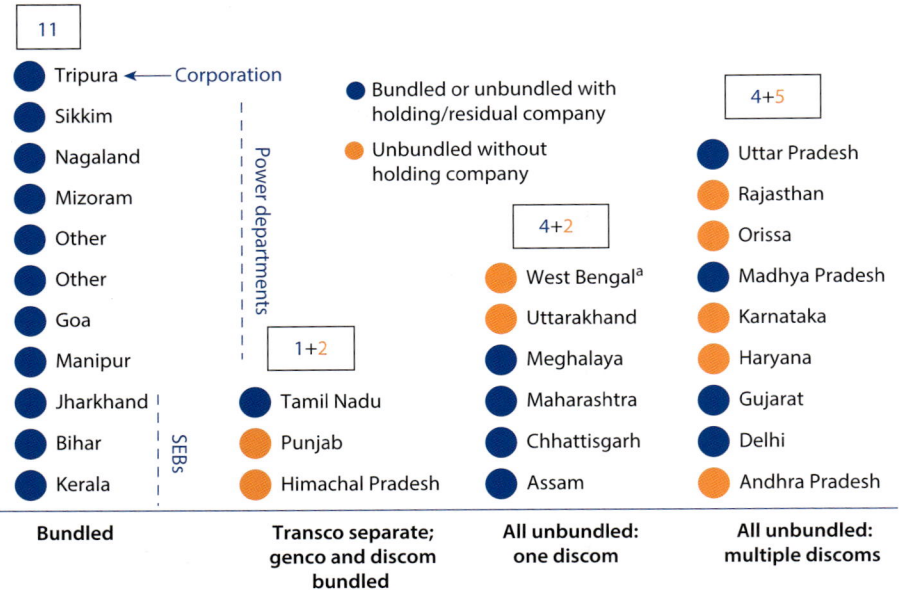

Source: Based on Government of India data.
Note: Discom = distribution company; genco = gemeration company; transco = transmission company.
a. West Bengal's hydro generation is still bundled with its discom, but thermal generation is in a separate company.

Even after unbundling, several states still follow practices that limit company separation and potentially inhibit independent functioning, suggesting that utilities in unbundled states do not always function independently. Where multiple utilities still depend on a holding company, decision making remains centralized across them. Other aspects that undermine separation include the continued existence of a single staff cadre for all utilities in the state, as described above, centralized cash flows, lack of autonomous cash management, lack of independence in financing decisions, and absence of independent power procurement.

Unbundling is therefore perhaps better thought of as a continuum rather than a discrete state. Utilities may be separate entities legally but may still make operational decisions—procurement, human resources, information technology (IT), and regulatory responses—together, receive common direction from a holding company, and make financial decisions as a single entity. The closer a utility is to having financial and operational independence, the more likely it is that the impacts that are thought to come from unbundling—accountability, transparency, and, ultimately, stronger performance—will be observed. This may explain why, in a simple categorization of unbundling, unbundled utilities represent both some of India's worst and best performers.

Corporate Governance Requirements for State Utilities in India

Indian state-owned power utilities are exempt from many of India's CG requirements, as those only apply to centrally owned or listed companies. Instead, they are required to follow the Companies Act, which stipulates only basic provisions on board size and meeting frequency; the total number of directorships any director can hold and the remuneration directors may receive; the constitution and composition of an audit committee; and guidelines for preparing annual reports, financial statements, and audited accounts.[4]

India has, though, extensive guidelines on CG developed over the past 15 years or so. In 1998, driven by the conviction that good CG was necessary for Indian firms to be able to access global and domestic capital at competitive rates, the Confederation of Indian Industry developed a voluntary code of CG. The code was well received, and some progressive companies adopted it; however, it was felt that a statutory code would be more purposeful and meaningful in the Indian context.

Thus in 2000, the Securities and Exchange Board of India (SEBI) made the provisions of the Confederation's code mandatory for listed companies through Clause 49 of its Listing Agreement. SEBI emphasized the importance of shareholder rights and the role of the board as an agent of the owners: CG relies on the "acceptance by management of the inalienable rights of shareholders as the true owners of the corporation and of their own role as trustees on behalf of the shareholders" (SEBI 2003, 1). In 2007, the Department of Public Enterprises (DPE) created similar guidelines for central public sector enterprises, which became mandatory in 2010. The guidelines set out by SEBI and the DPE go well beyond the Companies Act and, while generally considered recommended practices for Indian state-owned firms, are not mandatory for utilities owned by state governments.

The DPE guidelines are most applicable to state-owned utilities, as they cover government-owned companies (albeit central rather than state). This review, therefore, uses them as the benchmark for recommended practices. Their main provisions are as follows:

- *Board Composition.* Executive or "full-time" directors[5] should constitute no more than 50 percent of the board. There should be no more than two government representatives, and such directors should constitute less than one-sixth of the board. If the chair is a nonexecutive (executive) director, at least one-third (50 percent) of the board should be independent directors.[6] Neither the DPE nor SEBI provides guidance on the number of "promoter" directors (box 3.2).
- *Board Functioning.* Boards should meet at least four times a year, with no more than three to four months between any two meetings. They should conduct peer evaluations of nonexecutive board members.
- *Audit Committee.* Every board should have an audit committee with at least three members, two-thirds of whom, including the chair, must be

Box 3.2 Types of Directors

Executive Director: Director who is a utility employee.
Government Director: Director who is a government employee.
Independent Director: Director not associated with utility, government, or owner.
Promoter Director: Director who represents the interests of the promoters—that is, controlling shareholders or owners (of private holding company, for example).

---

independent directors. All members should be able to read and understand basic financial statements.
- *Government-Board Relationship.* There should be clarity about where the board has decision-making powers and where the board must seek government approval.

Appendix A lists the CG requirements specified by SEBI and the DPE in more detail.

In 2011, the Shunglu Committee, set up by the Planning Commission to identify steps to improve the performance of SEBs and distribution companies, recognized that deeper restructuring of the sector was warranted.[7] Making the same link as earlier with utility performance, its recommendations made explicit reference to improving regulatory and corporate governance in states, albeit in the context of the organizational changes necessary to modernize the sector (box 3.3).

Most recently, perhaps acknowledging the benefits of bringing other stakeholders formally into the governance framework for state utilities, the Government of India's Scheme for Financial Restructuring of State Distribution Companies (October 2012) has suggested bringing lenders' representatives on to boards of directors as nominees. To avoid rekindling concerns about the opposing interests of debt and equity holders, lenders might benefit from, instead, nominating an independent director to the board. Currently, there are no nominees of financial institutions on the boards of state utilities in India.

Findings—Corporate Governance in Practice

This review of CG is based upon basic data obtained from a large sample of utilities and detailed qualitative data obtained from a smaller set of utilities. The detailed data were obtained from management of 21 utilities in 14 states, as well as from the regulators and relevant government departments in those states.[8] The detailed sample comprises 12 distribution companies (discoms), 7 transmission companies (transcos), 1 generation company (genco), and 1 holding company. It takes a close look at the relationship between state governments and utility boards, the composition and functioning of the boards, and the utilities' management practices. As data availability varies across questions, with utilities often

---

Box 3.3 Shunglu Committee Recommendations on Corporate and Regulatory Governance

- **Board Composition and Function**
  - CEO who also serves as full-time chair for fixed 3–5 year term
  - CEO/chair and full-time board members selected transparently by a selection committee under merit-based open competition from across India
  - Two independent directors (at least) with relevant experience from the power sector

- **New Organizational Culture**
  - Human Resources
    - Encourage voluntary retirement to reduce overstaffing and allow recruitment of professional staff with appropriate skills and training
    - Provide strong support, from top management down, for in-house information technology (IT)
    - Bring in modern management and IT skills (especially among senior and middle management)
  - Finance and Audit
    - Finance department staffed with professionals with appropriate certifications
    - Computerized accounts enabling automatic inter-unit reconciliation
    - Accountability for actual recovery of arrears with close monitoring and penal actions specified
    - Work toward private participation through distribution franchises or minority flotation

- **State Government**
  - Political and administrative support for loss reduction; Planning Commission to monitor progress
  - Transparent agricultural subsidies: reduction in subsidies over time if state does not pay utility what is due

- **Regulator**
  - Independent from state government
  - Performance to be independently monitored
  - Utility boards to closely monitor quality and timeliness of utility submissions to regulators

---

more forthcoming with positive than negative data, the sample size for the different variables changes, and some measures may be upwardly biased.

The basic CG data were obtained from an additional 48 utilities in the original 14 and 5 additional states: 25 discoms (including 2 joint discom–gencos), 8 transcos, 14 gencos, and 1 corporation that performs all three electricity functions.[9] Overall, data were collected for 69 of the 89 utilities that the Power Finance Corporation covered in its 2010–11 report. Appendix B lists all of the utilities included in the review—including the full name of each utility as well as relevant abbreviations.[10] Sample sizes are indicated in the figures or text; when not stated, the sample comprises all 69 utilities.

The main finding of this review is that, while most utilities are in compliance with the basic governance requirements of the Companies Act, significantly fewer follow the guidelines laid out by the DPE or the Shunglu Committee that would be considered good practice for Indian utilities. For example, though almost all utilities have an audit committee, only 28 percent have an independent director heading it. Similarly, almost all have boards of between 3 and 12 members,[11] but less than one-third follow the suggested restriction on government directors, less than one-fourth have a chairman and managing director (CMD) lasting on average more than three years, and only 14 percent have the recommended percentage of independent directors on the board. Also, only 56 percent have any other specialized board committees. Finally, few boards have put the necessary processes in place to support their governance structures. Fewer than half the utilities have an advanced management information system (MIS), and no utility has a corporate performance monitoring system. Only about one-quarter of utilities consider merit when making promotion decisions, and only half have a well-defined employee training policy.

External Accountability

External accountability covers features of the relationships of the government (as owner), the regulator, and the general public with the utility represented by its board.

As noted, for state-owned corporatized enterprises, the role of the board is delicate. On the one hand, as the owner's agent it monitors management; on the other, it has a fiduciary responsibility to insulate management from political pressures and ensure that business decisions are taken on their merits. The history of state control of SEBs means that the autonomy of the board and its ability to operate without government interference is particularly important for corporatized state power utilities. However, state governments often continue to exert informal influence over utility decisions even after corporatization, and, in many cases, there are significantly more government directors on utility boards than recommended. As a natural consequence of the latter, there are often fewer than recommended independent directors on the boards to mitigate government influence.

The regulator is the other major external entity holding the utility accountable for performance. This relationship, too, must be managed appropriately, including addressing the legitimate interest of the public in key utility information that should be disclosed, such as basic company data, organization charts, company rules, budget allocations, and accounts.

By 2011, all states had established independent state electricity regulatory commissions (SERCs), technically separating the government's ownership and regulatory roles. However, as discussed in chapter 4, state governments select the SERC chair and members, have approval authority over hiring additional SERC staff, can issue "directions" to the regulator, and often exert informal influence over SERC decisions—all of which blur the limits of the state's role.

Government and Board

All state governments have consolidated utility ownership: utilities report to each state's Department of Power or Energy, which acts as the nodal department for all other interactions between the utility and the state government. Generally the government, as owner, oversees a nominations committee that approves every appointment to the board and has the sole power to remove directors. In every state, however, the government also selects and removes utility CEOs, rather than leaving this to the board, which is the common practice in most private firms. Political interference in utility appointments and decision making is more likely in these circumstances.

State governments directly appoint government officials ("government directors," typically members of the state power department) to utility boards—the DPE guidelines limit centrally owned companies to two such directors and recommend that they represent no more than one-sixth of a board's strength. Only about a quarter of the electricity utilities reviewed follow this practice (figure 3.2): 49 of 69 utilities have more than two government directors, and government directors make up over one-sixth of the board in all but 2 utilities (West Bengal's discom and Maharashtra's discom). Three utilities (Chhattisgarh's discom, genco, and transco) have boards composed entirely of government directors. On average, government officials constitute 48 percent of electricity utilities' boards.

Utilities' articles of association generally specify the areas where the board has independent decision-making powers. However, informal consultations often occur on a range of issues in different states, sometimes even covering areas in

Figure 3.2 Utilities with More than Two Government Directors

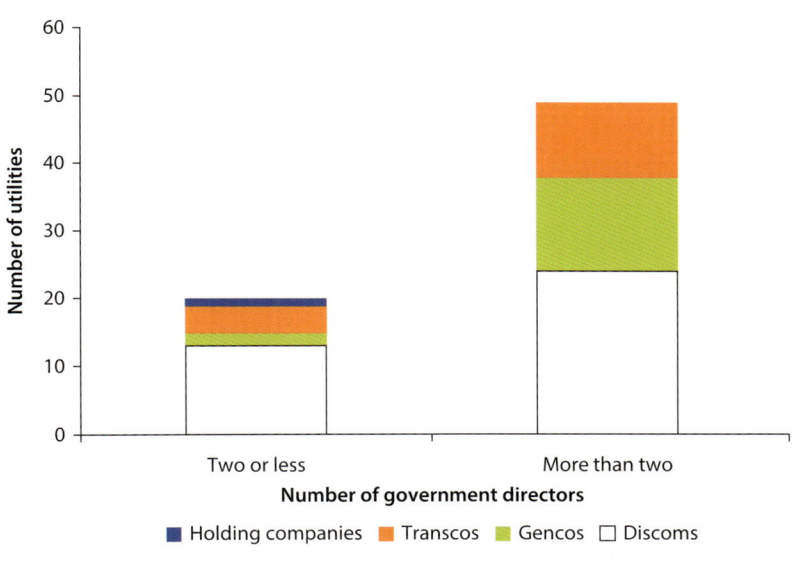

Source: World Bank compilation.
Note: Discom = distribution company; Genco = generation company; Transco = transmission company.

which the board should act independently. In addition, some utilities' articles grant the state government explicit rights to issue directives.[12] Most of the 22 utilities interviewed indicated that the government participates—formally and informally—in key decisions and policy matters, including the filing of tariff petitions, recruitment and promotion decisions, and other routine matters (such as procurement and decisions on enforcement) (figure 3.3).[13] Only Tata Power in Delhi (the only private company in the sample of utilities interviewed in detail), DGVCL (a discom) and GUVNL (a holding company) in Gujarat, and the three utilities in West Bengal reported no government involvement in any of these areas.

A few utilities in the sample are joint ventures between a state government and a private entity, including Tata Power Delhi (TPDDL), BSES Rajdhani Power Limited (BRPL), and BSES Yamuna Power Limited (BYPL), all of which are jointly owned by the Delhi government and private holding companies, as well as three of the four distribution utilities in Orissa, which are joint ventures between the government of Orissa and a private entity. In all these cases, the promoters—that is, controlling shareholders or owners (here, the private holding companies)—directly appoint directors to the board to represent their interests as promoter directors. As with government directors, these directors represent the interests of the owner, but they are unlikely to have the same interest in state government policy priorities as government directors do.[14] Promoter directors represent 27 percent of board strength in TPDDL, 14 percent in BRPL and BYPL, and 44 percent in each of the three Orissa utilities.

Active independent directors—ideally from the private sector and with reputations to protect—can help bring new ideas and awareness of external developments to the board. Having no material interest in the utility, they are likely to be unbiased and unmotivated by self-interest in their role of strategic advisors and vigilant monitors of management.[15] They also usually have a commercial orientation that is more focused on performance than on government loyalties.

Recommendations on the number and share of independent directors on the board vary, from a minimum of two in the Cadbury and Shunglu Committee reports to a minimum of between one-third and one-half of the board in the DPE guidelines. About 39 percent of sampled utilities have at

Figure 3.3 Government Involvement in Different Utility Decisions

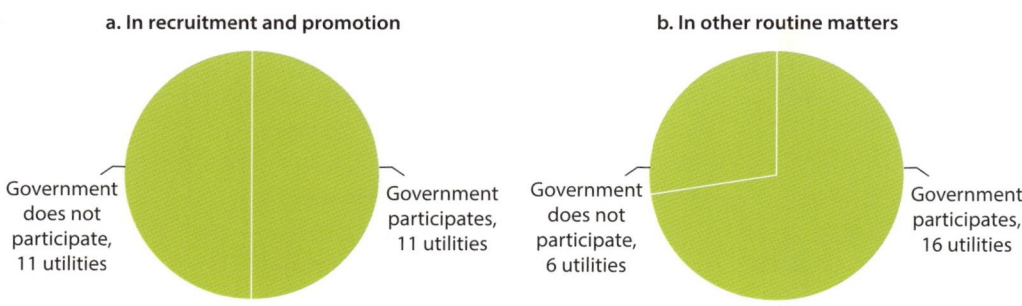

Source: World Bank compilation.

least two independent board members, but only 14 percent of utilities have enough independent directors to comply with the DPE guidelines, including utilities in Assam, Gujarat, Haryana, Madhya Pradesh, Orissa, and Uttarakhand. Among utilities that comply with the DPE guidelines, independent directors account for 39 percent of the board (figure 3.4). Surprisingly, 31 utilities (45 percent of the sample) do not have any independent directors on their boards, including those in Chhattisgarh, Gujarat, Haryana, Karnataka, Maharashtra, Orissa, Punjab, Rajasthan, Tripura, and Uttar Pradesh.

State governments track utility performance as well as progress in achieving key goals such as the level of village or household electrification. Achievement of goals is assessed through parameters like power supply position, utilization of funds from government programs, technical and commercial losses, commissioning and implementation of transmission projects, and overall profit and loss. These parameters are typically monitored through periodic meetings conducted by the Chief Minister or Minister for Power or Power Secretary, though in some cases governments have established mechanisms for utilities to submit this information themselves. Most states have much scope for improving the reliability and timeliness of the information they submit.

Regulator and Board

An effective utility board also needs to have a strong relationship with the regulator (who sets utility tariffs among other things). This ensures that the utility understands and meets the regulator's expectations in its annual revenue requirement (ARR) and tariff filings and that the regulator understands the financial data in those filings. An initial indication of the seriousness with which the board

Figure 3.4 Utilities with Board Share of Independent Directors Meeting DPE Guidelines

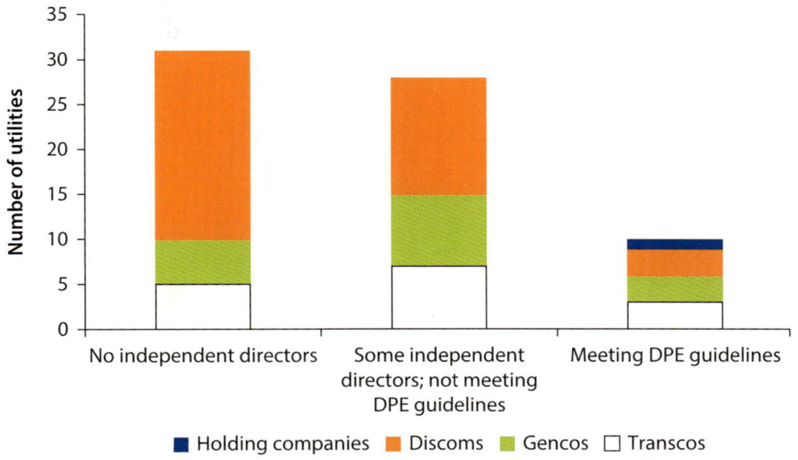

Source: World Bank compilation.
Note: DPE = Department of Public Enterprises; Discom = distribution company; Genco = generation company; Transco = transmission company.

takes its relationship with the regulator is whether the board has a dedicated regulatory cell: only 13 do not (figure 3.5).

Accountability to the Public
The Companies Act mandates the use of an external auditor; all 69 utilities in the sample comply. The DPE guidelines encourage, though do not require, utilities to make their annual accounts and audit reports public. Slightly more than half of the sample publish their accounts on their websites (over half of discoms, almost all gencos, and just under half of transcos), but only 42 percent of the sample publish audit reports on their websites.

The Companies Act also requires firms to finalize their annual accounts within six months of the end of the fiscal year. Of the 57 utilities that answered this specific question, 49 (86 percent) do so (figure 3.6).[16]

Internal Accountability
Boards of directors have two major roles: setting the company's strategy and policies and monitoring managers' performance. The primary focus of board deliberations is on the business merits of decisions on investment, human resources, and commercial and strategic aspects (Clarke 2005). With state-owned utilities, boards also seek to insulate management (and decision making) from political interference. To really improve performance, however, the board needs to be able to hold management accountable, and thus requires information systems that generate data for monitoring management in real time and that create incentives for improving performance. In addition, as managerial accountability for performance increases, utilities can be expected to re-engineer business processes to improve management control and customer services.

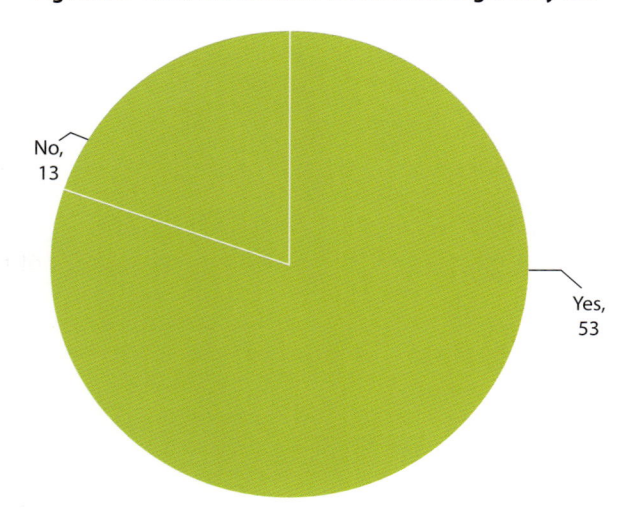

Figure 3.5 Utilities That Have a Dedicated Regulatory Cell

No, 13

Yes, 53

Source: World Bank compilation.

Figure 3.6 Utilities That File Their Accounts on Time and Make Accounts and Audit Reports Public

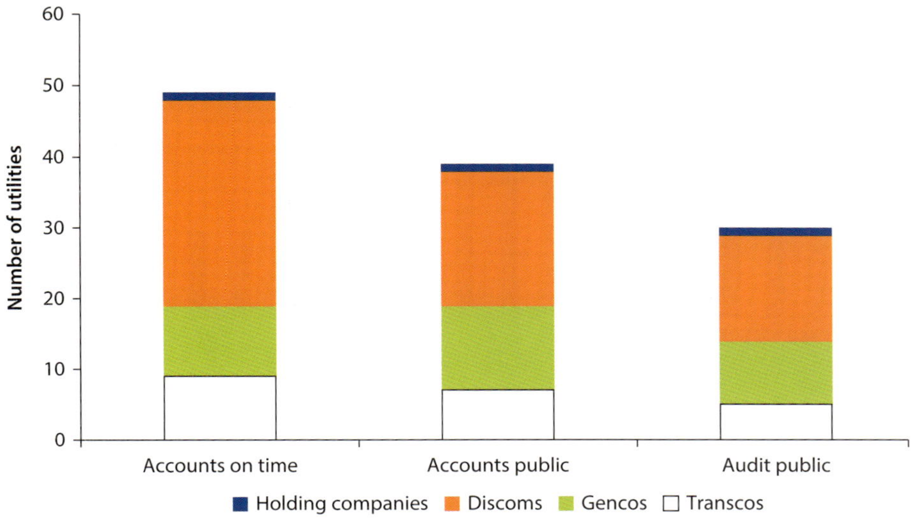

■ Holding companies ■ Discoms ■ Gencos ☐ Transcos

Source: World Bank compilation.
Note: Discom = distribution company; Genco = generation company; Transco = transmission company.

The rest of this chapter presents findings, from the utilities studied, on board functioning; features of the relationship between the board and management; and management practices.[17]

Board Composition and Internal Processes

Board effectiveness in its monitoring role is determined by its independence, size, and composition, with independence closely related to composition, particularly the number and percentage of board members accounted for by outside (independent) directors. Effectiveness also depends on the discipline imposed on top management by CEOs, with CEO turnover an important indicator of the ability to bring such discipline to bear (John and Senbet 1997).

A longer tenure for the board chair is recommended to provide stability in direction and the ability to see through the implementation of initiatives. The Shunglu Committee, for example, recommends that the chairs have fixed 3–5-year tenures. Data on tenure were available for 41 utilities; of those, 9 have average tenures (measured since utility inception) within the Shunglu Committee's 3–5-year range, 24 have average tenures of 1.5–2.5 years, and the remaining 8 have average tenures of less than 1.5 years. The average chair tenure over the past 5 years over all utilities sampled is 2.2 years (figure 3.7).

The fact that the chairpersons of most utility boards are Indian Administrative Service (IAS) officers who move frequently from post to post may be one reason for lower than optimal tenures. Such IAS presence may well have led to short-termism and a disinclination to take on difficult projects with

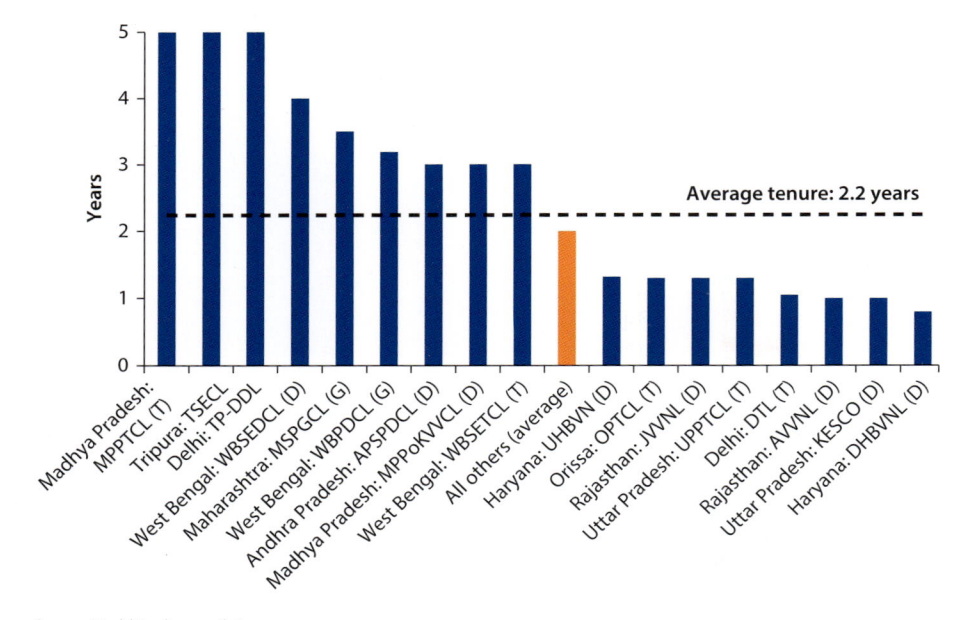

Figure 3.7 Average Chairperson/Managing Director Tenure

[Bar chart showing average tenure in years for various utilities, with an average tenure line at 2.2 years]

- Madhya Pradesh: MPPTCL (T): 5
- Tripura: TSECL: 5
- Delhi: TP-DDL: 5
- West Bengal: WBSEDCL (D): 4
- Maharashtra: MSPGCL (G): 3.5
- West Bengal: WBPDCL (G): 3.2
- Andhra Pradesh: APSPDCL (D): 3
- Madhya Pradesh: MPPoKVVCL (D): 3
- West Bengal: WBSETCL (T): 3
- All others (average): 2
- Haryana: UHBVN (D): 1.3
- Orissa: OPTCL (T): 1.3
- Rajasthan: JVVNL (D): 1.3
- Uttar Pradesh: UPPTCL (T): 1.3
- Delhi: DTL (T): 1.05
- Rajasthan: AVVNL (D): 1
- Uttar Pradesh: KESCO (D): 1
- Haryana: DHBVNL (D): 0.8

Source: World Bank compilation.
Note: (D) = discom; (G) = genco; (T) = transco.

longer-term payoffs. Another possible drawback is that IAS officers tend to be generalists and operate in a network and culture likely to impede development of a true business orientation (Tongia 2003). This is potentially exacerbated by the political sensitivity of the bureaucracy, borne out of its close interaction with the political class.[18] However, a broad strategic vision and practical implementation experience are arguably more important in a chief executive than deep technical expertise, so the generalist nature of IAS officers may actually be an advantage.

Of 44 utilities with data, 38 have a chair from the IAS.[19] Commentators have noted that the predominance of IAS officers as heads of utilities, chairpersons of regulatory commissions, and, of course, government functionaries makes the separation of roles and the emergence of truly independent entities (both regulatory and, potentially, corporate) difficult.[20]

The board is more likely to be effective if the board itself is not too large so that all members have a voice.[21] The Companies Act requires that boards have at least three directors. Beyond that, guidelines do not specify specific sizes but recommend that smaller is better. Other documents held up as best practice (such as the West Bengal Articles of Association) specify a limit of 12 board members. Among India's state power utilities, board size ranges from four (in all three of Chhattisgarh's utilities and Uttar Pradesh's discom—MVVNL) to 15 (in Karnataka's transco), with just over half of the 69 utilities concentrated in the 7–9 range (figure 3.8). The average board size across all utilities sampled is 8.2.

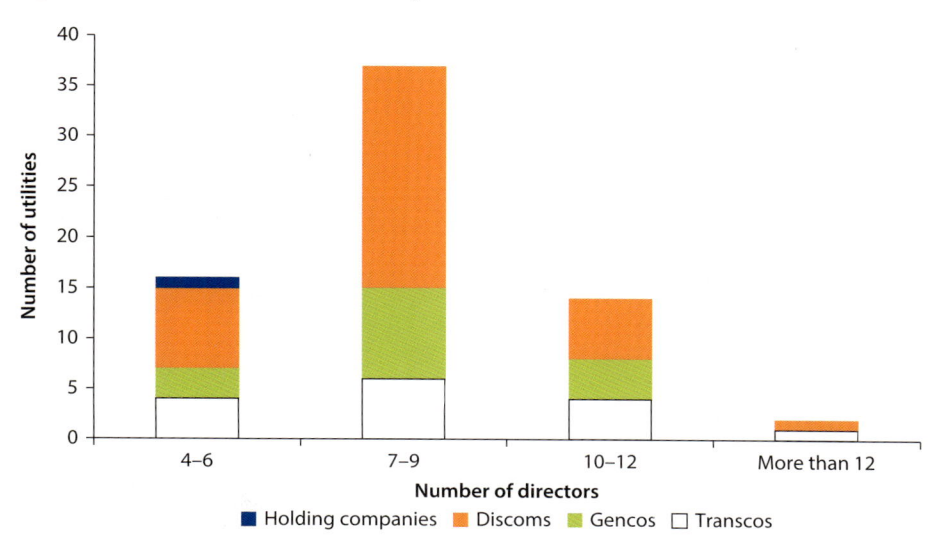

Figure 3.8 Number of Directors on Utility Boards

Source: World Bank compilation.
Note: Discom = distribution company; Genco = generation company; Transco = transmission company.

The board is best able to do its job if members understand their roles and responsibilities, share a common strategic vision, and operate in the firm's best interest. For this, training is important, as are peer review and transparency in procedures. None of the 21 electricity utilities surveyed conducts training for their directors, despite strong recommendations from the DPE, OECD, and others. No utilities in the "detailed" sample conduct appraisals or peer evaluations of their board members, nor are utility boards explicitly evaluated by state-government owners. West Bengal's transco and TPDDL both have codes of conduct for directors, and West Bengal's discom was preparing one when this review was written. Data on other utilities are unavailable.

The Companies Act and the DPE specify a minimum number of board meetings per year—generally four, with no more than three months between any two. Of the 13 utilities for which data are available, all meet the minimum requirement, with meetings per year ranging from four (Uttar Pradesh's discom—MVVNL—and transco) to 16 (Rajasthan's discom—JVVNL) (figure 3.9). On average, the 13 utilities have 7.85 meetings annually.

Board and Management

The literature on CG emphasizes the benefits of separating the board's monitoring and strategic/advisory functions—often by using specialized committees for each function (Adams and Ferreira 2005). Of the 55 utilities that provided these data, 44 percent do not have any specialized committees (other than the mandated audit committee). The remainder indicated that they have some specialized committee(s), covering, for example, procurement/purchases, human resources and recruitment, project appraisal and monitoring, technical

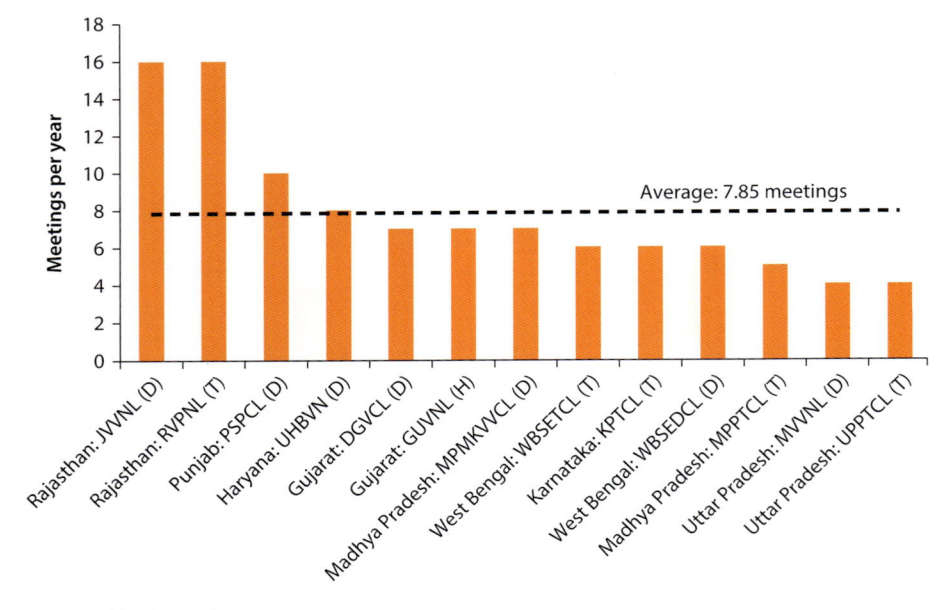

Figure 3.9 Average Number of Board Meetings per Year

[Bar chart showing meetings per year with a dashed line at Average: 7.85 meetings. Bars from left to right:
- Rajasthan: JVVNL (D): 16
- Rajasthan: RVPNL (T): 16
- Punjab: PSPCL (D): 10
- Haryana: UHBVN (D): 8
- Gujarat: DGVCL (D): 7
- Gujarat: GUVNL (H): 7
- Madhya Pradesh: MPMKVVCL (D): 7
- West Bengal: WBSETCL (T): 6
- Karnataka: KPTCL (T): 6
- West Bengal: WBSEDCL (D): 6
- Madhya Pradesh: MPPTCL (T): 5
- Uttar Pradesh: MVVNL (D): 4
- Uttar Pradesh: UPPTCL (T): 4]

Source: World Bank compilation.
Note: (D) = distribution company; (G) = generation company; (H) = holding company; (T) = transmission company.

aspects, operations review, borrowing/finance/balancing and settlement, risk management/revenue protection, power coordination and trading, and business ethics.

The Companies Act requires all companies, including utilities, to have an audit committee as a key mechanism of internal accountability. Of the 69 utilities for which we have data, 93 percent have established audit committees (figure 3.10). Five utilities (all three of Chhattisgarh's utilities, Tripura's state corporation, and Uttar Pradesh's UPJVNL genco) do not have audit committees.[22] The academic literature on CG and the DPE CG guidelines recommend that the audit committee be headed by an independent director. Fewer than one-third of utilities reporting (10 of the 36 for which data are available) have an independent director chairing the audit committee (figure 3.11). This includes three of Andhra Pradesh's four discoms, Assam and Orissa's gencos, DGVCL in Gujarat, Haryana's transco, and all three of West Bengal's utilities.

The DPE guidelines suggest that no more than half of all board members should be executive directors, as boards with a preponderance of executive directors function de facto as a management committee. Of the 69 utilities in the sample, 80 percent comply with this, with executive directors constituting 27 percent of the board on average among utilities that comply (figure 3.12). For the rest—primarily discoms in Andhra Pradesh, Himachal Pradesh, Karnataka, Maharashtra, Punjab, Tamil Nadu, Tripura, and Uttar Pradesh—executive directors constitute 68 percent of the board on average.

Figure 3.10 Utilities with Audit Committees

No, 5
Yes, 64

Source: World Bank compilation.

Figure 3.11 Utilities with an Independent Director Chairing the Audit Committee

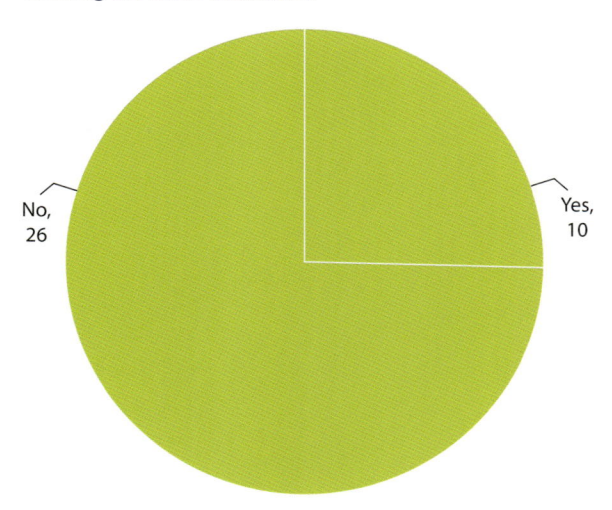

No, 26
Yes, 10

Source: World Bank compilation.

Management Practices

As noted, to make well-informed decisions, boards need to have accurate information, ideally coming from utility-wide IT-enabled systems. Whether utilities have an enterprise resource planning (ERP) system or advanced MIS is a reasonable proxy for whether a board has access to adequate information. Of the 46 utilities that answered this question, about 40 percent have an ERP system or advanced MIS (figure 3.13), including all four of Andhra Pradesh's

Figure 3.12 Utilities with Executive Directors Constituting Less or More than Half of Board Members

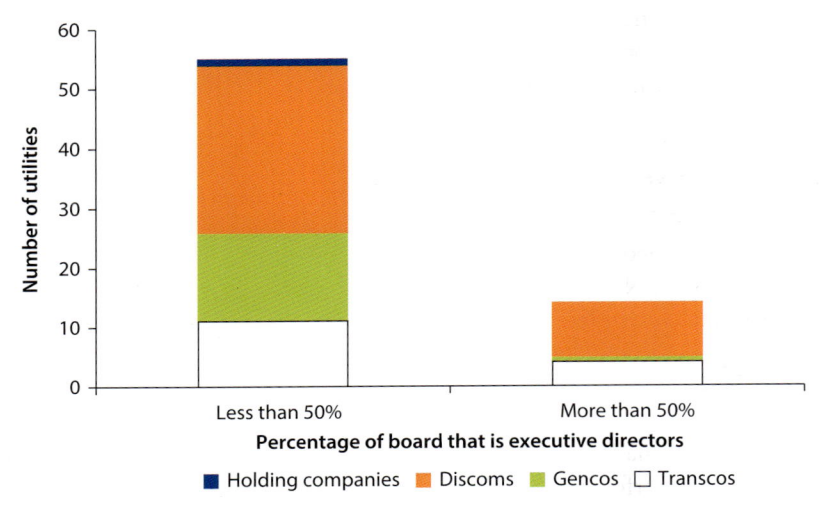

■ Holding companies ■ Discoms ■ Gencos ☐ Transcos

Source: World Bank compilation.
Note: Discom = distribution company; Genco = generation company; Transco = transmission company.

Figure 3.13 Utilities with an ERP System or Advanced MIS

No, 27
Yes, 19

Source: World Bank compilation.
Note: ERP = enterprise resource planning; MIS = management information system.

discoms, all six of Delhi's utilities, Gujarat's DGVCL discom and its holding company (GUVNL), Himachal Pradesh's SEB, Karnataka's transco, Maharashtra's discom, and one of Madhya Pradesh's discoms.[23] The central government's Restructured Accelerated Power Development and Reform Programme to increase efficiency of distribution provides significant support for adoption of IT for key functions and has been instrumental in prompting progress in this area.

Well-run corporations use corporate performance management systems to monitor organizational performance according to predetermined key performance indicators. The process is linked to organizational mission, vision, and strategic objectives. None of the utilities surveyed has a corporate performance management system. The West Bengal discom stands out as the one utility that has tried to institute one, initially on a manual basis with a vision of later tying it to an IT system. However, the pace of implementation has suffered from lack of staff interest and little management commitment.

It is generally recommended that boards establish a policy on hiring and promotion that encourages staff performance in furthering the utility's goals. DGVCL and GUVNL in Gujarat (a discom and holding company, respectively) and Delhi's Tata Power (a private discom) stand out as the only utilities surveyed[24] that have instituted performance-linked incentives for employees. Six utilities have a promotion policy based at least in part on merit, though TPDDL is the only one whose promotion policy is primarily merit-based (others also heavily weigh seniority). Finally, 11 utilities have well-defined employee training policies. Only three have performance-linked incentives, merit-based promotion policies, and training policies—TPDDL, DGVCL, and GUVNL—a feature that may be partly responsible for these utilities' relatively strong performance.

Overall

The indicators collected for this review can be aggregated into two CG indexes— a "basic" index, with coverage of 67 of the 69[25] utilities, which indicates the degree to which utilities have adopted eight standard CG good practices; and a "detailed" index across 18 indicators including the eight standard practices as well as indicators on internal processes and relationship with the government. The detailed index is only available for the 21 utilities giving detailed qualitative information. Index scores are calculated as the percentage of total indicators for which the utility complies with the recommended practice.

Consistent with the broad findings above, utilities score relatively well on the basic index, but almost all of those in both indexes score much less well on the detailed index. Appendix C shows each utility's compliance with the indicators included in the basic and detailed (if available) indexes, and Appendix D presents the data points underlying the indexes.

The indicators included in the basic index, with recommended practice indicated in parentheses, are (table 3.1): number of government directors on the board (≤ 2), independent directors as share of total number of directors on the board (≥ 33 percent, or ≥ 50 percent if the chairperson is an executive member of the board), executive directors as share of total number of directors on the board (≤ 50 percent), board size (≤ 12), having an audit committee, and following recommended audit practices (publishing accounts publicly, publishing audit reports publicly, and using an external auditor).

The 67 utilities covered by the basic index on average comply with 61 percent of the DPE and other recommended practices included in the index. The lowest compliance is 38 percent (Tripura's corporation, Uttar Pradesh's UPJVNL genco,

Table 3.1 Share of Utilities in Compliance with Indicators That Constitute the Basic Index

Indicator	Utility receives a 1 if…	Share of sample meeting this (%)	Sample size	Number of utilities meeting criterion
External accountability				
Independent directors	>= 33% or ≥ 50% if chairperson is executive	15	67	10
Government directors	≤ 2	28	67	19
Audit made public	Yes	45	67	30
Accounts made public	Yes	58	67	39
Use an external auditor	Yes	100	67	67
Internal accountability				
Executive directors	≤ 50%	81	67	55
Board size	≤ 12	97	67	65
Have an audit committee	Yes	93	67	62
Overall (basic index)		61	67	

Source: World Bank compilation.

TANGEDCO in Tamil Nadu, and Karnataka's MESCOM discom), while two utilities (Assam's discom and Gujarat's holding company) achieve full compliance. Twelve utilities—about 18 percent of the sample—comply with all but one of the indicators (all 12 miss the same indicator: they all have more than two government directors).

The detailed index includes, in addition to the basic indicators listed above, indicators on internal processes and the relationship with the government—in particular, the existence of other specialized board committees, having an independent director heading the audit committee, preparing annual accounts on time, having an average CMD tenure of at least three years, lack of government influence over routine and recruitment decisions, existence of an ERP system or advanced MIS, use of performance-linked incentives, consideration of merit in promotion decisions, and existence of a clearly defined employee training policy.

Among the 21 utilities with detailed information, five stand out as following at least two-thirds of recommended CG practices: Gujarat's discom (DGVCL) and holding company, West Bengal's discom and transco, and Tata Power in Delhi (table 3.2).

These five utilities are also among the stronger financial or operational performers in India. For example, DGVCL and Tata Power are among the five discoms with the lowest aggregate technical and commercial losses in India, and DGVCL, Tata Power, and West Bengal's discom are among the six discoms with the highest profit per unit of energy purchased.

This connection between strong CG and performance could be due to a variety of factors, including the positive impact of strong governance practices on profit and efficiency, or that more profitable firms tend to adopt better CG measures for a range of reasons. Boxes 3.4–3.6 look in more detail at West Bengal's utilities, Tata Power, and Gujarat's utilities to highlight good practices and lessons.[26]

Table 3.2 Characteristics of the Top Five Utilities Covered in the Detailed Index

		Gujarat (DGVCL)	Gujarat (GUVNL)	West Bengal (WBSEDCL)	West Bengal (WBSETCL)	Delhi (Tata Power)
		Discom	Holding company	Discom	Transco	Discom
Board-management relationship	% of board that is executive directors	14	33	50	50	9
	Audit committee	Y	Y	Y	Y	Y
	Other committees	Y	Y	Y	Y	Y
	Independent head of audit committee	Y	N	Y	Y	N
	Audit on time	Y	Y	Y	Y	Y
Public accountability	Audits made public	Y	Y	Y	Y	N
	Accounts made public	Y	Y	Y	Y	N
Board effectiveness	Number of directors on board	7	6	12	8	11
	Average CMD tenure (years)	2.3	2.8	4.0	3.0	5.0
External accountability	Number of government directors	3	2	2	2	5
	% of board that is independent directors	43	33	33	25	18
	Government influences routine matters	N	N	N	N	N
	Government influences recruitment	N	N	N	N	N
	Use an external auditor	Y	Y	Y	Y	Y
Management practices	ERP/MIS	Y	Y	N	N	Y
	Performance-linked incentives	Y	Y	N	N	Y
	Employee training policy	Y	Y	Y	Y	Y
	Merit-based promotions	Y	Y	Y	Y	Y

Source: World Bank compilation.
Note: CMD = chairman and managing director; Discom = distribution company; ERP = enterprise resource planning; MIS = management information system; N = no; Transco = transmission company; Y = yes.

Box 3.4 Corporate Governance as an Instrument of Change in West Bengal

By 2002, years of inefficient operation of transmission and distribution had led to annual losses of around US$300 million in West Bengal's power sector. The state government decided to restructure the sector and implement measures to enhance accountability, anticipating that this would lead to improved performance outcomes and a lower burden on the exchequer. By 2007, it had unbundled its state electricity board (SEB) into separate generation, transmission, and distribution utilities (though hydropower generation remained with the discom).

As in many states, the government took on SEB liabilities in the unbundling process. But, unique to West Bengal, the government mandated utility compliance with India's corporate governance (CG) requirements for listed companies (Clause 49 of the Securities and Exchange

box continues next page

Box 3.4 Corporate Governance as an Instrument of Change in West Bengal *(continued)*

Board of India's Listing Agreement) as a condition of the transfer scheme. The new utilities were to be run by their boards of directors without interference by the state so long as they did not request budget support from the government. This meant, for example, that recruitment and procurement would not require the state government to sign off, and this remains the agreement today. (With state governments currently faced with bailing-out utilities, there is a valuable opportunity to follow West Bengal's model.)

These agreements established utilities with robust governance practices and gave them the space needed to establish core operating principles under the guidance of strong independent directors brought on to the utility boards at their inception. Once the utilities were observed to work with financial and operational efficiency,[a] these operating principles became firmly entrenched and have remained largely undisturbed—despite a major change in the state's political governance.

The articles of association of state utilities in West Bengal mirror these agreements. They set out a clear process for director selection and removal, give specific direction on the board's powers, establish a fixed tenure (a minimum of three years) for directors, and limit the board to 12 members. Other advantages: having a well-defined director selection process helped prevent the board being stacked with political appointees who might have lacked business acumen and the necessary technical background (though this could have been strengthened by defining selection criteria); specifying tenures provided stability and certainty, ensuring that directors would be present long enough to have an impact; and limiting board size protected against a lack of focus.

West Bengal also used to good effect its government officers' knowledge of global best practices in power reform. While it was obvious that "one size does not fit all," reformers presented examples of the success of new operational models to advocate for change with employee organizations and political executives. This is considered to have enabled reforms such as putting in place objective employee performance assessments and performance-linked promotion and compensation. Employee resistance was also low because a long hiring freeze meant that the reorganization would lead to better prospects for career growth. In addition, this allowed the utilities to re-skill fairly painlessly.

Importantly, West Bengal's state electricity regulatory commission is one of the few to consistently raise tariffs to cover the cost of supply, increasing tariffs each year from FY08 to FY11. Tariff increases came to a halt in FY12 under a new state government but resumed more recently, reportedly in part because the state utilities made a compelling case to the new government that its constituents were willing to pay more for the consistent and reliable power that higher tariffs enable.

a. Significant operational changes included implementation of computerized billing, 100 percent feeder metering, strict monitoring and vigilance to prevent theft, and near-100 percent consumer metering.

Box 3.5 Corporate Governance in a High Performing Joint Venture—Tata Power (Delhi)

Before 2002, Delhi had a power system that suffered from aggregate technical and commercial (AT&C) losses of 50–60 percent and rampant power cuts under a vertically integrated State Electricity Board (SEB) that required heavy government subsidies each year to meet revenue shortfalls. To improve performance, the state government unbundled the SEB in 2002, dividing the distribution function into three companies. It then entered into joint ventures with private parties, who bid for 51 percent of the equity of each of these new companies with the winner selected on the basis of promised loss reductions.

Tata Power was awarded one of these companies—North Delhi Power Limited, later renamed Tata Power Delhi Distribution Limited (TPDDL). A variety of technological (meter replacement, automated meter reading, outage management systems, network planning software) and social interventions (publicity on the need to pay for electricity, corporate social responsibility initiatives) were implemented by the joint venture. The utility greatly improved its operational and financial performance: AT&C losses fell from 53 percent in 2002 to 11 percent in 2012; average system availability increased by nearly 42 percent; and the transformer failure rate came down to less than 1 percent.

On corporate governance, the near-equal public and private ownership of TPDDL is largely reflected in its board composition (five nominee directors from the government of Delhi and three promoter directors from the holding company, Tata Power). The board rates highly on measures of effectiveness and has a raft of supporting board committees (such as Operations Review Committee, Remuneration Committee, Business Review Committee, and Long-Term Loans and Borrowings Committee) in addition to an Audit Committee. The utility has an external auditor and the board follows a code of conduct and ethics. Every director has access to all the utility's financial and operational information and, despite its being a joint venture, there has been no government influence on the utility's functioning, management, or decision making. The tenure of the chairman and managing director is five years.

Box 3.6 Organizational Transformation and a Turnaround in Performance in Gujarat

In 2000, Gujarat Electricity Board (GEB) was one of the worst performing power utilities in India, a drag on the government's finances and on the state's development. A decade later, in 2010, the GUVNL group, comprising seven interlocked companies, is a model public utility, winning awards for innovation and customer service. It is efficient, agile, and profitable.

New political leadership initiated the turnaround. While power purchase remained centralized even after GEB was unbundled, there was real decentralization of authority and decision making to the unbundled companies, each with its own corporate office and a professional board. Politicians were replaced by bureaucrats and professionals on the boards of GUVNL,

box continues next page

Box 3.6 Organizational Transformation and a Turnaround in Performance in Gujarat *(continued)*

the holding company, as well as its constituent units, while the very best generalist-administrators were appointed to the top management of the unbundled utilities. Strong political backing was given to discom staff, including in matters such as preventing power theft by the politically connected.

A multipronged change management strategy was put in place. It involved a campaign of information, education, and communication with all staff and stakeholders reminding them about the goal, how the organization was progressing, and how the staff and stakeholders could contribute to it; using dialogue to jointly develop solutions to issues raised by staff; incentivizing improved housekeeping practices to increase revenues and cut costs; and implementing initiatives to improve utility finances by cutting transmission and distribution losses and theft. The government neutralized employee apprehensions by signing a tripartite agreement with GEB management and employee unions that working conditions would be no worse, that no jobs would be shed, nor any employee relocated without consent. Starting off the new entities with a clean balance sheet also made achievable the financial sustainability of the new structure. A transformation of work culture was accomplished by investing heavily in training and capacity building of all staff from the chairman and managing director to the lineman.

The management of the GUVNL group also set about strengthening driving forces for change—implementation of e-Urja, an enterprise resource planning platform, for example, became instrumental in developing a strong information and communications technology culture, that has, in turn, empowered staff to develop homegrown solutions to their problems. Decentralized decision making empowered even junior field staff; competition among discoms contributed to galvanizing employees around corporate goals, and a culture of performance management around key performance indicators further enhanced staff participation. For instance, to curb farmers stealing power from single-phase supply by using phase-splitting capacitors, distribution company engineers designed special transformers that trip whenever the load exceeds a given limit.

Source: Shah and others 2012.

On the detailed index, the 21 utilities on average follow recommended practices for only 46 percent of the indicators included. In contrast, these utilities complied, on average, with 67 percent of the indicators in the basic index. Table 3.3 presents performance on this index, overall and by subtopic. Also included in the table, for comparison, is each utility's score on the basic index.

Table 3.4 presents the correlation between different CG variables. As would be expected, the share of the board accounted for by different types of directors is significantly correlated: a higher percentage of independent directors is quite naturally related to lower levels of executive and government directors, and a strong negative relationship is observed between the shares of government and executive directors as well.

Chapter 5 takes a closer look at the possible link between strong CG practices and utility financial and physical performance.

Table 3.3 Utility Performance on the Detailed Index

State	Utility	Type	Detailed index (%)	Basic index (%)	Board-management (%)	Public accountability (%)	Board effectiveness (%)	External accountability (%)	Management practices (%)
Gujarat	GUVNL	Holding company	**89**	**100**	88	100	50	100	100
Gujarat	DGVCL	Discom	**89**	**88**	100	100	50	75	100
West Bengal	WBSEDCL	Discom	**78**	**88**	100	100	100	75	50
West Bengal	WBSETCL	Transco	**78**	**88**	100	100	100	75	50
Delhi	Tata Power	Discom	**67**	**50**	83	0	100	50	100
Maharashtra	MSPGCL	Genco	**61**	**75**	75	100	100	50	50
Maharashtra	MSEDCL	Discom	**56**	**75**	83	100	50	25	25
Madhya Pradesh	MPMKVVCL	Discom	**56**	**63**	63	0	50	50	50
Karnataka	KPTCL	Transco	**56**	**63**	88	100	0	0	75
Assam	APDCL	Discom	**44**	**100**	63	100	50	50	0
Assam	AEGCL	Transco	**44**	**88**	67	100	50	25	0
Andhra Pradesh	APCPDCL	Discom	**44**	**75**	63	100	50	25	25
Madhya Pradesh	MPPTCL	Transco	**44**	**63**	67	0	100	50	25
Delhi	DTL	Transco	**44**	**50**	67	0	50	25	50
Rajasthan	RVPNL	Transco	**33**	**63**	63	100	50	0	0
Rajasthan	JVVNL	Discom	**33**	**50**	63	0	50	0	0
Punjab	PSPCL	Discom	**33**	**50**	50	0	50	25	0
Haryana	UHBVN	Discom	**28**	**50**	50	0	50	0	0
Uttar Pradesh	UPPTCL	Transco	**28**	**50**	38	0	50	25	0
Uttar Pradesh	MVVNL	Discom	**22**	**50**	25	0	50	25	0
Tamil Nadu	TANGEDCO	Discom	**22**	**38**	38	0	50	0	0

Source: World Bank compilation.
Note: The bold values are scores on the indexes that have been created. Discom = distribution company; Genco = generation company; Transco = transmission company.

Table 3.4 Correlation among Corporate Governance (CG) Variables

	Number of directors	CMD tenure	Basic CG index	Detailed CG index	% of board that is independent directors	% of board that is executive directors	% of board that is government directors
Number of directors	1						
CMD tenure	−0.0865	1					
Basic CG index	0.0458	0.1113	1				
Detailed CG index	0.1671	0.4858**	0.6999***	1			
% of board that is independent directors	0.1689	0.2077	0.5915***	0.5556***	1		
% of board that is executive directors	−0.0904	−0.0407	−0.0268	0.4282*	−0.2514**	1	
% of board that is government directors	−0.0788	0.278*	−0.2870**	−0.0934	−0.4196***	−0.6680***	1

Source: World Bank analysis.
Note: CG = corporate governance; CMD = chairman and managing director. The CMD tenure row and column only show correlations for the 41 firms covered; the Detailed CG index row and column only show correlations for the 21 firms covered.
Significance level: * = 10 percent, ** = 5 percent, *** = 1 percent.

Notes

1. OECD 2005. Also see "Overview of the Corporate Governance ROSC Program," World Bank, www.worldbank.org/ifa/rosc_cgoverview.html.
2. Major corporate scandals, such as Enron and WorldCom's accounting frauds, highlight the importance of strong corporate governance (CG) practices—independent oversight, the avoidance of conflicts of interest around accounting procedures, accurate and transparent reporting to both directors and shareholders—in ensuring that companies are run in accordance with shareholders' interests (Coffee 2002; Elson and Gyves 2003; Rosen 2003; Clarke 2005).
3. In Assam, the chairs of the transco and discom sit on each other's boards.
4. Key Companies Act requirements used in this review are that companies must have a minimum of three members on their boards; there should be an audit committee, with a minimum of three members, two-thirds of whom must not be executive or managing directors; and the board must meet at least once every three months.
5. Sometimes known as "functional" directors, executive directors are typically drawn from senior management of the company (such as directors of finance or of human resources).
6. An independent director is one who, apart from receiving director's remuneration, does not have a financial relationship with the company; is not related to persons occupying high-level management positions; has not been a senior executive or managerial personnel of the utility in the preceding three years; is not a partner of the utility's statutory audit firm, legal firm, consultants, or other experts that have material associations with the utility; and is not a substantial shareholder of the utility.
7. http://planningcommission.nic.in/reports/genrep/index.php?repts=hlpf.html.
8. The 14 states were selected to ensure a range of locations and sizes. Utilities within the states were selected to include at least one discom and at most one other utility. Within that, selection was based upon ease of access to senior management and

likelihood of data availability. These decisions were all made in view of the difficulty and time intensity of obtaining CG data.

9. For simplicity, when statistics are given by utility-type, Tripura State Electricity Corporation Ltd. is categorized as a discom. In addition, detailed reviews were undertaken of practices in six distribution utilities: Assam Power Distribution Company Ltd., Dakshin Gujarat Vij Company Ltd., West Bengal State Electricity Distribution Company Ltd., Madhya Pradesh Madhya Kshetra Vidyut Vitaran Company Ltd., Jaipur Vidyut Vitaran Nigam Ltd., and Andhra Pradesh Central Power Distribution Company Ltd.

10. Combining the detailed sample and the additional utilities for which basic data were collected, the full sample comprises 37 discoms, 15 transcos, 15 gencos, 1 corporation, and 1 holding company.

11. The upper limit of 12 is taken from the Articles of Association of the West Bengal utilities, commonly considered a good model.

12. For example, the Articles of Association of Uttarakhand Jal Vidyut Nigam Ltd. (UJVNL) state: "The Govt. of Uttarakhand may from time to time issue directive(s) to the company as to the exercise and performance of its functions in matters involving the security of the State or substantial public interest and to the finances and conduct of business and affairs of the company. … The company shall give immediate effect to the directive(s) so issued" (https://www.upcl.org/wss/downloads/RtiManuals_pdfs/Manual-4.pdf, accessed July 15, 2013).

13. Information on this aspect was obtained for one utility from the broader sample in addition to the set of 21 utilities covered in the detailed sample.

14. In the case of state-owned utilities, a promoter director (such as an appointee or employee of the holding company) is unlikely to have different incentives or interests from a government director, so the analysis does not differentiate between the two.

15. Another view is that independent directors tend to have poorer information than insiders, so may be unable to monitor management as effectively as government or executive directors. See Adams and Ferreira (2005) and Harris and Raviv (2008).

16. Utilities that do not include Assam's discom and genco, Chhattisgarh's discom and transco, Kerala's SEB, Tripura's state corporation, and Uttar Pradesh's transco and one of its discoms.

17. The information presented is oriented toward governance structures due to the difficulty of obtaining what is often considered confidential information on internal company practices.

18. Sunil Mitra, former Secretary Power West Bengal, private communication.

19. The few data do not permit an unequivocal answer on the impact on utility financial performance of having an IAS officer as CMD.

20. Dubash and Rao 2006. In some cases, the state's Energy Minister is appointed board chair, which makes the utility particularly susceptible to political influence. We are indebted to Shantanu Dixit for this observation.

21. In addition, documents need to be prepared and circulated to all members in advance, and the agenda needs to be kept to important issues.

22. This is technically a violation of the Companies Act associated with penal provisions; however, companies usually apply for and obtain waivers granting additional time for compliance.

23. Madhya Pradesh's two other discoms and Orissa's transco were adopting such systems at the time of writing this review.

24. Of the 21 utilities surveyed in depth.
25. Two transcos (GRIDCO in Orissa and PSTCL in Punjab) lacked sufficient data for inclusion in the index.
26. While deeper analysis of the political economy of change would be required to come to a definitive conclusion, it is instructive that the initial impetus for change in these three states (including the privatization of distribution in Delhi) appears to have come from the government/political leadership. In all three cases, the fiscal burden of a poorly performing power sector and consumer unhappiness with constant power cuts seems to have created the political will to take steps not only to improve the situation but to turn the sector into a source of comparative advantage for the state.

References

Adams, Renee B., and Daniel Ferreira. 2005. "A Theory of Friendly Boards." Finance Working Paper 100, European Corporate Governance Institute, Brussels.

Adams, Renee B., Benjamin E. Hermalin, and Michael S. Weisbach. 2009. "The Role of Boards of Directors in Corporate Governance: A Conceptual Framework and Survey." *Journal of Economic Literature* 48 (1): 58–107.

Black, Bernard, and Vikramaditya Khanna. 2007. "Can Corporate Governance Reforms in Increase Firms' Market Values: Evidence from India." *Journal of Empirical Legal Studies* 4: 749–96.

Cadbury Committee on the Financial Aspects of Corporate Governance. 1992. *Report of the Committee on the Financial Aspects of Corporate Governance*. London: Burgess Science Press.

Clarke, Thomas. 2005. "Accounting for Enron: Shareholder Value and Stakeholder Interest." *Corporate Governance: An International Review* 13: 598–612.

Coffee, John C. Jr. 2002. "Understanding Enron: It's about the Gatekeepers, Stupid." Columbia Law and Economics Working Paper 207, New York.

Dubash, Navroz K., and Narasimha Rao. 2006. "Emergent Regulatory Governance in India: Comparative Case Studies of Electricity Regulation." Presented at "Frontiers of Regulation: Assessing Scholarly Debates and Policy Challenges," University of Bath, U.K., September 7–8.

Elson, Charles M., and Christopher J. Gyves. 2003. "The Enron Failure and Corporate Governance Reform." *The Wake Forest Law Review* 38: 855.

Fagernas, Sonja. 2006. "How Do Family Ties, Boards, and Regulation Affect Pay at the Top? Evidence for Indian CEOs." Working Paper 335, Centre for Business Research, University of Cambridge, Cambridge, U.K.

Fields, M. Andrew, and Phyllis Y. Keys. 2003. "The Emergence of Corporate Governance from Wall St to Main St: Outside Directors, Board Diversity, Earnings Management, and Managerial Incentives to Bear Risk." *Financial Review* 38 (1): 1–24.

Ghosh, Saibal. 2006. "Do Board Characteristics Affect Corporate Performance? Firm-Level Evidence for India." *Applied Economic Letters* 13 (7): 435–43.

Harris, Milton, and Artur Raviv. 2008. "A Theory of Board Control and Size." *Review of Financial Studies* 21 (4): 1797–832.

Hermalin, Benjamin E., and Michael S. Weisbach. 2003. "Boards of Directors as an Endogenously Determined Institution: A Survey of the Economic Literature."

Working Paper Series, University of California–Berkeley, Center for Responsible Business, Berkeley, CA.

John, Kose, and Lemma W. Senbet. 1997. "Corporate Governance and Board Effectiveness." NYU Working Paper FIN-98-045, Stern Department of Finance, New York University.

OECD (Organisation for Economic Co-operation and Development). 2005. *OECD Guidelines on Corporate Governance of State-Owned Enterprises*. Paris: OECD Publishing.

Rosen, Robert. 2003. "Risk Management and Corporate Governance: The Case of Enron." *Connecticut Law Review* 35 (1157).

SEBI (Securities and Exchange Board of India). 2003. *Report of the SEBI Committee on Corporate Governance: February 8, 2003*. Mumbai, India.

Shah, Tushaar, Madhavi Mehta, Gopi Sankar, and Shankar Mondal. 2012. "Organizational Reform in Gujarat's Electricity Utility: Lessons for Revitalizing a Bureaucratic Service Delivery Agency." IWMI Water Policy Research Highlight 6, International Water Management Institute, Colombo, Sri Lanka.

Tongia, Rahul. 2003. "The Political Economy of Indian Power Sector Reforms." Working Paper, Program on Energy and Sustainable Development, Stanford University, Stanford, CA.

Vagliasindi, Maria. 2008. "Governance Arrangements for State Owned Enterprises." Policy Research Working Paper 4542, World Bank, Washington, DC.

Wong, Simon C. Y. 2004. "Improving Corporate Governance in SOEs: An Integrated Approach." *Corporate Governance International* 7 (2).

CHAPTER 4

Regulatory Governance

The establishment of state electricity regulators under the 1998 Electricity Regulatory Commission Act, and, subsequently, the Electricity Act of 2003 (EA 2003) (which superseded it) was intended to reduce government control over the power sector and to de-link it from electoral politics.[1] The EA 2003 aimed to create an independent, unbiased, and transparent governance framework that balanced consumer and investor interests, specifically by removing regulation and tariff determination from the purview of the government.[2]

However, the performance of the sector has remained lackluster, leading to questions about the de facto accountability and independence of the state electricity regulatory commissions (SERCs) and their role in developing and maintaining an operating environment that creates incentives for long-term efficient operation while meeting service delivery targets:

> Most state governments have approached the reform of the sector in a half-hearted fashion. For example, they have been reluctant to grant autonomy to their power utilities, contriving to retain management control or influence through top level appointments, even where they are unbundled and corporatized. ... Similarly, most state governments have met the federal legal requirement to establish regulatory commissions, but have given them very limited jurisdiction. Even in states where regulators have been given a wider mandate, questions arise about their independence, process of appointment, and powers of enforcement (Lal 2006, 11).

Another issue is that almost all state-level power utilities in India remain state owned, removing the market context for independent regulation and raising questions about the extent to which a regulator can even influence the actions of a state-owned utility, since "to have effective regulations, you must have utilities that can, in fact, be regulated" (Berg 2013). Berg notes that "[b]oth sector regulators and state-owned water utilities are formal organizations embedded in a social structure. The fundamental problem is whether one governmental entity (a regulatory commission or a municipal council) can influence the actions of another governmental entity that delivers water services (which may be at the national or subnational level). In particular, the utility might 'bypass' the regulator, by drawing upon an alliance with the line ministry responsible for the water services sector."[3] Also, regulators can only infrequently apply sanctions to utilities because they generally have less political weight than utilities.

The institutional framework determines whether the regulator can have a positive impact on performance, but state ownership may limit the effectiveness of standard regulatory mechanisms, which would need to be adapted to the objectives and incentive structure of public enterprises. For state-owned utilities, economic sustainability is balanced against stated social objectives and (generally unstated) political objectives (Berg 2013). In privately owned utilities, shareholders are concerned about the impact of regulatory decisions on the return to their equity and the board holds management accountable for performance through bonuses, salaries, hiring, and firing. But in state-owned utilities, there is often little concern about return on equity; bonuses are rare as are penalties for poor performance. While it is entirely possible for state-owned utilities to link incentives or penalties to performance, such a commercial orientation requires professionalism in the utility and insulation from political intervention—governance arrangements and associated managerial incentives are central to achieving high performance. In fact, "unless the internal governance of the utility focuses on performance (via pressure from the board of directors)" the regulator is unlikely to be able to improve performance (Berg 2013). Thus sound regulatory and corporate governance are reinforcing elements in utilities' operating environment.

In addition, the ability of SERCs to carry out their mandates depends on the technical, financial, and human resources available to them, their competence, their autonomy in decision making (including insulation from political pressures), and, finally, their accountability. The credibility, legitimacy, and, indeed, effectiveness of SERCs are enhanced to the extent that their mandate is well defined and they are transparent and participatory in their functioning.

The rest of this chapter reviews the structural and institutional features of SERCs across India in recognition of the importance of these arrangements in creating a stable and effective regulatory environment, with concomitant implications for utility performance (Stern and Holder 1999). It describes the mandates given to SERCs under the EA 2003 and the extent to which SERCs have implemented them, as well as key institutional design (ID) aspects such as SERC autonomy, capacity, transparency, and accountability, which are expected to boost their effectiveness.

Mandates of SERCs

SERCs are mandated with multiple roles: to prevent political interference in the sector and to protect the interests of different stakeholders by regulating the operations of power utilities and the tariff chargeable to consumers (Prayas Energy Group 2003). Key responsibilities are to issue licenses for distribution and intrastate transmission; ensure nondiscriminatory open access (OA) to both the transmission and distribution systems in order to promote competition and support the development of a multibuyer market and power trading; regulate and rationalize tariffs so as to cover costs; implement multiyear tariff (MYT) frameworks to reduce uncertainty and encourage investment in the sector; establish and monitor standards with respect to quality and reliability of service by licensees; and safeguard consumer interests, including by setting up mechanisms to redress grievances (see box 4.1 for a full list). In addition, SERCs are tasked with drafting, notifying, and implementing a range of additional regulations to enact the mandates of the EA 2003.

Implementation of Regulatory Mandates

This section reviews the performance of SERCs grouped around the following elements of their mandates: tariffs, standards of performance, protection of consumer rights, and implementation of certain other regulations. Data were collected for all 28 SERCs, though data for three small states were patchy. In addition, in-depth reviews of regulatory practices were carried out for Andhra Pradesh, Assam, Delhi, Gujarat, Madhya Pradesh, and Maharashtra. Appendix E lists the SERCs covered in this review.

There has been solid progress, but most SERCs have not yet fully implemented the mandates given them in the EA 2003. For instance, tariffs cover average cost in the majority of states, but increases in tariffs have generally not kept pace with cost increases and very few states issue MYTs (despite issuing MYT regulations). Most SERCs are nominally complying with mandates to promote consumer empowerment and increase transparency to the public, but need to do far more to ensure that consumers are given opportunities to engage and that high-quality information is available to the public. Finally, though most SERCs have notified the key regulations necessary to enact the mandates of the EA 2003, in many cases they have yet to take concrete steps to actually implement these regulations.

Tariffs

In line with their most important mandate, most SERCs appear to set tariffs that would allow utilities to cover their costs, though the share of SERCs that accomplish this has declined over time. Delays in issuing tariff orders are common, there have been several years when many SERCs have not issued a tariff order at all, and tariff increases have generally not kept pace with cost increases. Only a few SERCs have notified an MYT framework and issued tariff orders under that framework (Delhi Electricity Regulatory Commission [DERC], for example).

Cost Recovery

In 2010, most SERCs set tariffs at a level that allowed utilities to recover their costs.[4] While cost recovery basically requires the tariff to equal or exceed average cost, a more stringent requirement is used in this review. Cost recovery is defined as the tariff level that covers (equals) average cost *plus* a premium to account for "normal" distribution losses, which are set at 10 percent for this analysis. Under this framework, an efficiently operating utility (one with normal distribution losses and 100 percent collection) that has a tariff equal to cost recovery, as

Box 4.1 SERC Responsibilities

The State Commission shall discharge the following functions, namely:

- determine the tariff for generation, supply, transmission, and wheeling of electricity, wholesale, bulk, or retail, as the case may be, within the State: Providing that where open access has been permitted to a category of consumers under section 42, the State Commission shall determine only the wheeling charges and surcharge thereon, if any, for the said category of consumers;
- regulate electricity purchase and procurement process of distribution licensees including the price at which electricity shall be procured from the generating companies or licensees or from other sources through agreements for purchase of power for distribution and supply within the State;
- facilitate intrastate transmission and wheeling of electricity;
- issue licenses to persons seeking to act as transmission licensees, distribution licensees, and electricity traders with respect to their operations within the State;
- promote cogeneration and generation of electricity from renewable sources of energy by providing suitable measures for connectivity with the grid and sale of electricity to any person, and also specify, for purchase of electricity from such sources, a percentage of the total consumption of electricity in the area of a distribution license;
- adjudicate upon the disputes between the licensees, and generating companies and to refer any dispute for arbitration;
- levy fee for the purposes of this Act;
- specify a State Grid Code consistent with the Grid Code specified under clause (h) of subsection (1) of section 79;
- specify or enforce standards with respect to quality, continuity, and reliability of service by licensees;
- fix the trading margin in the intrastate trading of electricity, if considered, necessary; and
- discharge such other functions as may be assigned to it under this Act.

The State Commission shall advise the State Government on all or any of the following matters, namely:

- promotion of competition, efficiency, and economy in activities of the electricity industry;
- promotion of investment in electricity industry;
- reorganization and restructuring of electricity industry in the State;
- matters concerning generation, transmission, distribution, and trading of electricity or any other matter referred to the State Commission by that Government.

Source: Electricity Act 2003, Section 86.

---

defined above, would break even.[5] "Operating cost recovery," similarly, is the tariff level that covers (equals) average operating cost plus a premium to account for "normal" distribution losses (10 percent here).

In 2010, 19 states had an average billed tariff high enough to cover their costs if utilities had sold all the energy purchased, while 17 of those states had an average tariff high enough to cover their costs even if utilities sold only 90 percent of energy purchased.[6] In reality, many of the 17 states with tariffs set at cost recovery, as defined above, did not generate enough revenue to cover their costs, either because their distribution losses were higher than 10 percent (they billed for less than 90 percent of input energy), they did not collect all the revenue they billed, or a combination of the two. In 10 states, tariffs were so low that utilities could not have recovered their costs even if they had sold all the energy purchased.

The analysis just above focuses on recovery of total costs, although the results are nearly identical if operating costs are considered instead (figure 4.1). While covering total costs is important, covering operating costs with tariff revenue is even more critical to operational sustainability. In 2010, 20 states had a tariff equal to or exceeding average operating cost and 18 states had tariffs equal to or exceeding operating-cost-recovery levels.

The number of states with tariffs achieving operating cost recovery has declined since 2003. Further, the ratio of the average billed tariff to the operating-cost-recovery level (the "operating-cost-recovery ratio") fell in the majority of states in 2003–10, suggesting that tariff increases generally failed to keep pace with cost increases (figure 4.2). In 2003, 25 states had tariffs above operating-cost-recovery levels, and 19 states had tariffs above total cost recovery levels. In 21 states, the operating cost-recovery ratio declined from 2003 to 2010. SERCs raised tariffs frequently (three or four times between 2007 and 2010, the period for which utility tariff revision data were available) in several of the states in which tariffs failed to keep pace with cost increases.

Figure 4.1 Ratio of Average Billed Tariff to Operating-Cost-Recovery Level and to Average Operating Cost, 2010

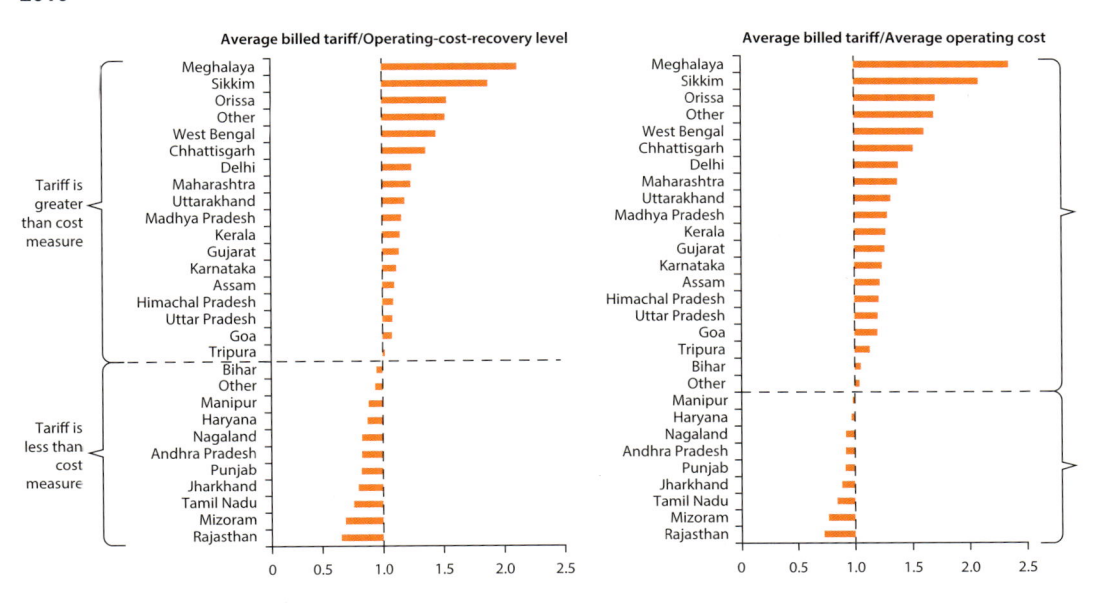

Source: World Bank compilation.

Figure 4.2 Change in Ratio of Average Billed Tariff to Operating-Cost-Recovery Level, 2003–10

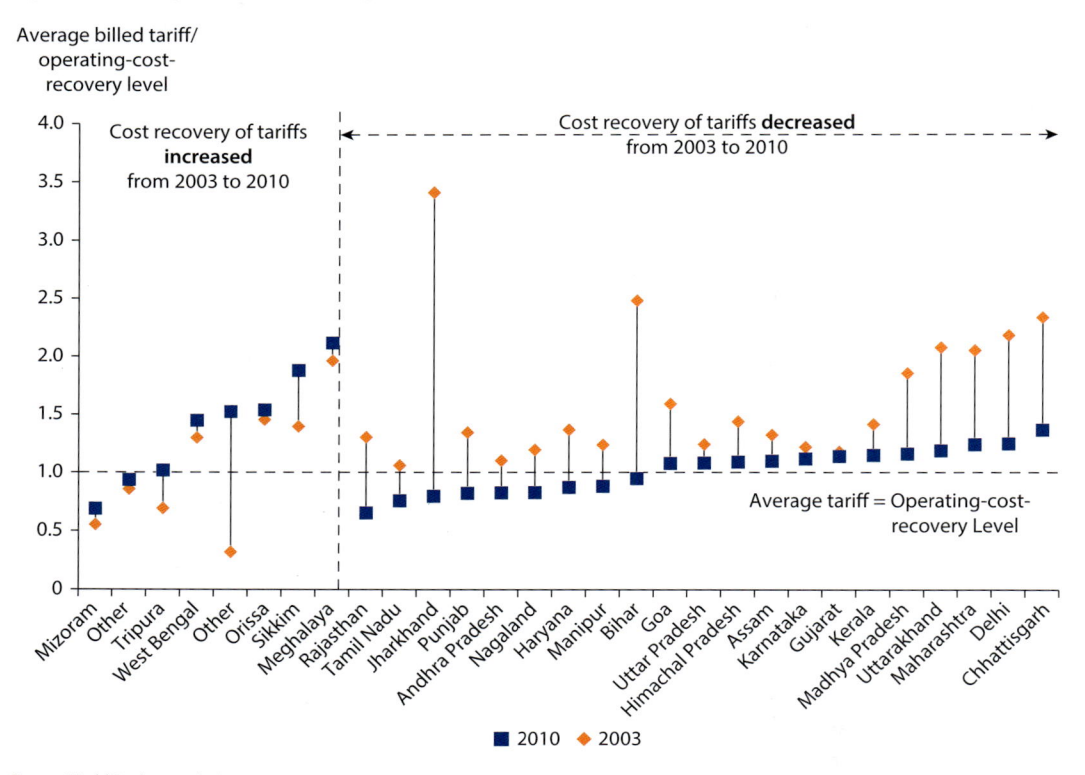

Source: World Bank compilation.

Tariff Revisions

From 2001 to 2010, only two state regulators (Andhra Pradesh and Haryana) issued a tariff order each year.[7] During this period the median share of years for which a tariff order was issued was 53 percent.[8] Eight SERCs (of the 25 with data) had one or more years in which they did not receive a tariff filing from every utility. Twenty SERCs failed to issue the tariff order within 120 days of receiving the utilities' annual revenue requirement (ARR) petitions (per EA 2003 requirements) at least once during 2008–10. The average delay in issuing a tariff order over the same three years was 213 days, with a minimum average delay of 30 days (Andhra Pradesh Electricity Regulatory Commission [APERC], which in most years issued the tariff less than 120 days after ARR receipt) and a maximum of 365 days (Goa, Nagaland, Punjab, and Tripura). The delays often arise because there are too few staff to handle the workload, sometimes because the workload itself is high on account of the large number of licensees to regulate. For example, Maharashtra Electricity Regulatory Commission (MERC) often faces delays in issuing its tariff orders as it handles the largest number of licensees and petitions of any state, and therefore requires far more discussion between the regulator and the licensees before finalizing the tariff.

Regular revisions in tariffs avoid the shock to consumers from having to adjust to a sudden large jump in the tariff. And they enhance the general acceptability of tariff increases and help prevent receivables, such as "regulatory assets," from building up in utility accounts.[9] Mounting regulatory assets in states such as Delhi, Haryana, Punjab, Tamil Nadu, Uttar Pradesh, and West Bengal have exacerbated their discoms' cash-flow problems, forcing them to borrow heavily to cover the deficit of revenues over costs (box 4.2).

SERCs have the leeway to determine the tariff on a *suo moto* basis even if the utility does not file an ARR; however, few SERCs actually take up cases in this manner, due to a combination of a lack of legislative clarity on when SERCs should initiate *suo moto* action and a lack of initiative among SERCs. Madhya Pradesh Electricity Regulatory Commission (MPERC) stands out as being proactive and has *suo moto* taken action in a number of cases. For example, MPERC passed the ARR and tariff order in FY06 even though none of the utilities in Madhya Pradesh had submitted tariff applications.

Tariff decisions can be challenged in the Appellate Tribunal, but this is relatively uncommon as seen in the fact that, although the average number of orders challenged for an SERC is just over five, the median is only three and the mode zero. Among the 20 SERCs that have had tariff orders challenged, only 38 percent of challenges have been successful, indicating that the Tribunal generally considers SERC orders satisfactory.[10]

Fifteen SERCs have issued MYT regulations, but only 10, including DERC and APERC, have actually issued an MYT order. (This is primarily due to a lack of historical data to provide a basis for projections and utilities' inability to accurately monitor and provide reports on key parameters necessary for updating the tariff.) The MYT framework provides greater certainty to potential investors since it specifies the path that tariffs will follow over time. By allowing utilities to retain a portion of the cost savings earned by "overachieving" transmission and distribution losses relative to the targets set by the Commission, the MYT framework also creates an incentive for licensees to improve performance.

On average, SERCs increased tariffs 1.5 times from 2008 to 2010. Six states increased tariffs each year over that period (Andhra Pradesh, Himachal Pradesh, Maharashtra, Meghalaya, Punjab, and West Bengal).[11] Nine states (Goa, Haryana, Jharkhand, Manipur, Mizoram, Nagaland, Rajasthan, Tamil Nadu, and Tripura) did not increase tariffs at all.

To properly set tariffs, SERCs need to conduct a cost of supply study to understand how much it actually costs to supply electricity to different categories of end-users; however, only five SERCs have ever conducted one—Himachal Pradesh, Gujarat, Delhi, Bihar, and Andhra Pradesh.[12] Such a study is also necessary to understand how much particular categories of consumers are being subsidized or are cross-subsidizing other categories of consumers. Without a detailed cost of supply study, SERCs must base the retail supply tariff on other estimates of cost.

Box 4.2 The Cost of Regulatory Assets

The tariff-setting mechanism, as currently worked out by the state electricity regulatory commissions (SERCs), is based on the annual revenue requirement (ARR), which includes a 16 percent post-tax return on equity as assured profit. An ARR is a detailed statement of expenditure in which a distribution company (discom) lists its proposed expenditure on network upgrades, purchase of equipment, and administrative and general expenses. The SERC scrutinizes each discom's ARR and fixes the tariff accordingly. Once the regulator has accepted the expenses leading to an agreed ARR, there is an implied tariff hike to be borne by consumers. At this point, the regulator may exercise discretion to create a so-called "regulatory asset": if it recognizes that a discom needs to be paid Rs 100 but feels this will burden consumers who can pay just Rs 60, Rs 40 is classified by the regulator as a regulatory asset, which is an outstanding receivable owed to the discoms on which 13–14 percent interest will be paid the following year as a carrying cost.

In 2013, the regulatory assets of the three Delhi discoms stood at Rs 70 billion (US$1.5 billion) with the interest on the principal mounting. If these regulatory assets are not liquidated, the interest burden will continue to rise and the utilities' financial position will become untenable, with an increasingly remote chance of recovering the full amount due since this would require unrealistically high tariff hikes. Government subsidies are likely to be required. If a solution to this problem is not found, there is a possibility of the discoms becoming cash-flow constrained to the point where, in cases like Delhi, private players could simply walk away from their investments.

While the Appellate Tribunal has said the carrying cost of regulatory assets should be paid to utilities every year to avoid cash-flow problems,[a] regulatory assets continue to pile up. In fact, regulatory assets have increased so sharply that utilities are unlikely to be able to retire them in three years. Delays in "truing up" add to the size of the regulatory assets—retail tariffs are always specified at the start of the year on the basis of the discom's expected operating costs, but if the costs and revenues are different from what is projected, these additional gaps are fixed by truing up the following year.

The regulatory assets problem is not confined to Delhi. Nationwide it is estimated that regulatory assets have reached over Rs 700 billion (US$15 billion) and that just the interest cost adds up to around Rs 95 billion (US$2 billion) each year. Discoms with mounting regulatory assets are facing increasing cash-flow problems, jeopardizing their functioning. Borrowing against regulatory assets is becoming less feasible: because commercial banks are unsure how to value regulatory assets that may not be worth their face value, discoms can no longer borrow up to the full amount of the regulatory assets they own. Other sources are required for funding discoms and there appears to be a strong case for providing them some relief, or at least liquidity.

a. Appellate Tribunal Order of 11 November 2011. The recovery of the regulatory asset should be time bound and within a period not exceeding three years at the most and preferably within the control period. The carrying cost of the asset should be allowed to the utilities in the ARR of the year in which the regulatory assets are created to avoid cash-flow problems for the distribution licensee.

Sources: ICRA 2012; Nair 2013; Sethi 2013.

Standards of Performance

All but two SERCs have notified regulations covering standards of performance (SoP). SoP typically cover aspects such as the time taken to release new connections, to restore supply after an interruption, and to resolve complaints over metering, billing, voltage fluctuations, and so on. All the notified regulations have clearly defined penalties for noncompliance,[13] but there is no monetary incentive for utilities to go beyond the minimum SoP.

About 80 percent of SERCs that have notified regulations report SoP results online. However, this approach does not necessarily imply the SERC is actively monitoring compliance. In some cases, SERCs publish performance reports received from utilities without verifying the authenticity of the data; moreover, there is no evidence of action taken on such reports, and only 75 percent of SERCs actually monitor compliance with the standards. Monitoring compliance is a challenge because licensees often do not have a system for measuring performance against the SoP.

SERCs in Madhya Pradesh, Gujarat, Delhi, Maharashtra, and Andhra Pradesh have been particularly successful in monitoring the compliance of distribution licensees with the SoP. These SERCs measure performance quarterly and publish annual compliance reports (in their local languages and English) in newspapers and online.

Low awareness of SoP among consumers and a limited ability to petition for compensation mean there is relatively little consumer pressure on utilities to perform. Some regulators have been proactive in attempting to overcome this barrier; for example, MERC publishes a Consumers' Rights Statement on its website. Possibly as a result of low consumer awareness, only two SERCs have ever issued penalties for noncompliance. Even in states with successful monitoring such as Madhya Pradesh, utilities have not generally compensated affected consumers when they have failed to meet the SoP.

Protection of Consumer Rights

Measures to protect consumer rights include establishment of consumer grievance-redressal forums (CGRFs), appointment of a consumer ombudsman, and creation of a state advisory committee (SAC). These requirements are nominally complied with by all SERCs. With the exception of a few stand-out SERCs (such as MERC, DERC, and Gujarat Electricity Regulatory Commission [GERC]), however, SERCs have put little effort into promoting consumer awareness and use of the CGRF and ombudsman (figure 4.3).

Consumer Grievance Redressal and Consumer Ombudsman

All but one SERC (Sikkim) have issued guidelines for utilities on setting up CGRFs. Utilities in all states but three have established CGRFs and all but four SERCs have a consumer ombudsman. GERC, which stands out in this area, has a four-tier system for redressal of consumer grievances, comprising consumer redressal committees at the division and circle levels, CGRFs at the corporate utility level, and a consumer ombudsman at the SERC level. GERC also recruits members of the CGRF from the public.

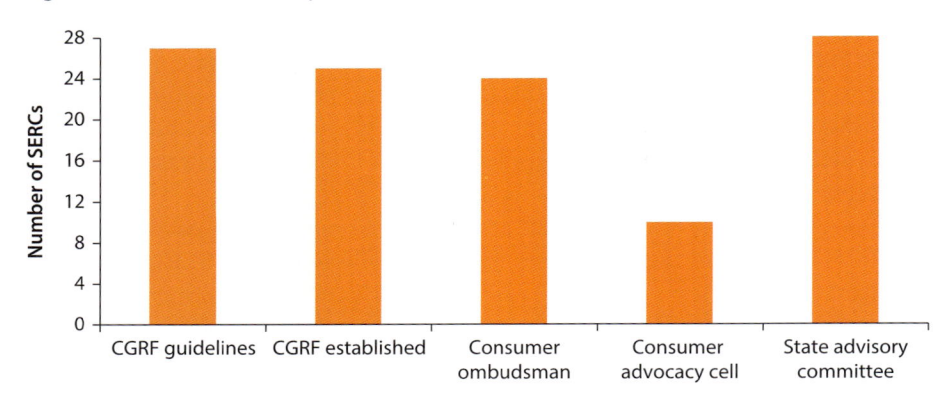

Figure 4.3 Measures Taken by SERCs to Protect Consumer Rights

Category	Number of SERCs
CGRF guidelines	27
CGRF established	25
Consumer ombudsman	24
Consumer advocacy cell	10
State advisory committee	28

Source: World Bank compilation.
Note: CGRF = consumer grievance-redressal forum; SERC = state electricity regulatory commission.

These steps are only preliminary, however, and SERCs need to make more effort to ensure that consumers are aware and able to leverage the benefits of these tools. Such steps can include establishing a consumer advocacy cell dedicated to increasing consumer awareness and assisting consumers in complaint redressal, and to putting online the status of complaints to the CGRF or ombudsman.

Ten SERCs have reported establishing consumer advocacy cells: Tamil Nadu, Orissa, Maharashtra, Madhya Pradesh, Kerala, Karnataka, Jharkhand, Delhi, Chhattisgarh, and Assam. This goes beyond what is mandated by the EA 2003. DERC, which stands out in this area, has appointed a dedicated Grievance Redressal Officer for consumers. Each year, around 400 grievances are received and resolved. This number indicates high awareness of regulatory issues among consumers in the state relative to others. In MPERC, the consumer advocacy cell consists of one person responsible for preparing and disseminating information for consumers, ensuring representation of consumers before the Commission, responding to and resolving consumer complaints, and advising in the case of wrong billing, noncompliance with performance standards, tariffs, and other related matters. MPERC stands out as one of the few electricity regulators to put online complaints made to the CGRF and ombudsman.

State Advisory Committees

All SERCs have established SACs that represent the interests of consumers and other stakeholders in the state and that advise SERCs in that respect. For example (among SERCs surveyed in detail), SACs in Delhi, Madhya Pradesh, Punjab, Gujarat, and Maharashtra represent the interests of agriculture, industry, commerce, nongovernmental organizations, academics, and individual consumers. SACs in Madhya Pradesh and Punjab also have representation from organized labor.

Suggestions from its SAC that the DERC has accepted include conducting consumer satisfaction surveys, regulating energy consumption of street lights, reducing cross-subsidies from industrial and other high-value consumers, and benchmarking the performance of Delhi against other states on distribution company costs. In Madhya Pradesh, some suggestions from the SAC that MPERC has accepted include establishing a separate tariff category for power-intensive industries, limiting the increase in minimum guaranteed consumption for nondomestic consumers, and introducing a formula for pass-through of unanticipated fuel price and other power procurement cost increases.

Other Regulations

Most SERCs have taken the first step of notifying key regulations mandated by the EA 2003—on average, SERCs have notified 8 of 11 key regulations. But few SERCs have fully implemented these regulations. For example, some states have yet to determine the tariffs for OA, despite having passed OA regulations. Perhaps as a consequence, only half the states have even received an OA application, and only 10 states have actually implemented OA for an applicant. Similarly, on renewable energy and energy efficiency, most states have notified basic renewable purchase obligation (RPO) regulations, but only 18 monitor compliance and only 4 have issued penalties for noncompliance. Far fewer states have passed demand-side management (DSM), feed-in-tariff (FIT), or time-of-day (ToD) metering regulations.

From the EA 2003 and related policies, SERCs need to notify regulations in the following 11 key areas: supply code, SoP, OA, metering, CGRF, trading, MYT, availability-based tariff (ABT), DSM and other energy efficiency promotion, ToD metering, and RPOs. On average, 7.8 regulations have been notified (the median and mode are both 8) (figure 4.4). No SERC has notified all 11, but five SERCs have notified 10 (Chhattisgarh, Gujarat, Himachal Pradesh, Maharashtra, and Rajasthan). Two SERCs have only notified one regulation; however, they became functional only one year before these data were collected.

The three most commonly notified regulations are OA, SoP, and RPOs, which have been notified by 27 of the 28 SERCs (figure 4.5). The least notified

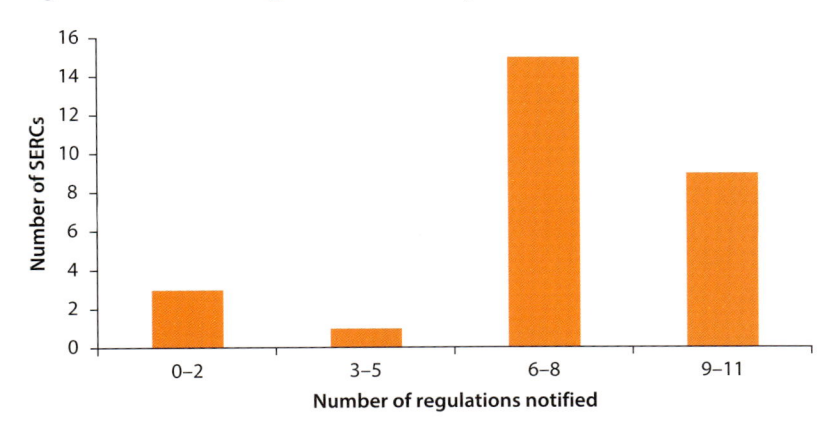

Figure 4.4 Number of Regulations Notified by SERCs

Source: World Bank compilation.
Note: SERC = state electricity regulatory commission.

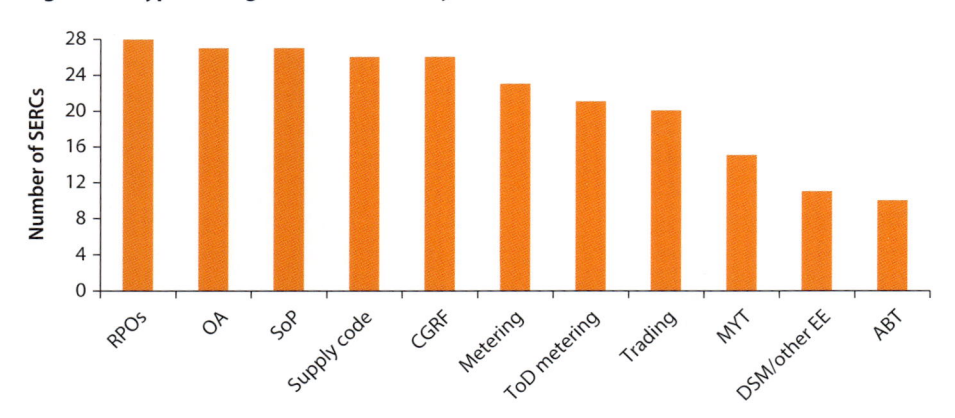

Figure 4.5 Types of Regulations Notified by SERCs

[Bar chart showing Number of SERCs for each regulation type:
- RPOs: 28
- OA: 27
- SoP: 27
- Supply code: 26
- CGRF: 26
- Metering: 23
- ToD metering: 21
- Trading: 20
- MYT: 15
- DSM/other EE: 11
- ABT: 10]

Source: World Bank compilation.
Note: ABT = availability-based tariff; CGRF = consumer grievance-redressal forum; DSM = demand-side management; EE = energy efficiency; OA = open access; SERC = state electricity regulatory commission; SoP = standards of performance; MYT = multiyear tariff; RPO = renewable purchase obligation; ToD = time-of-day.

regulations are intrastate ABT, DSM and other energy efficiency promotion measures, and MYT, which have been notified by only 10, 11, and 15 SERCs, respectively.

Most SERCs face significant challenges in ensuring that utilities comply with regulations and other directives (as noted for SoP, for example). MERC stands out here and, unlike other regulators, has ensured that licensees at least initiate action on its directives and regulations. In 2010–12, licensees initiated action on all the directives MERC issued.

The following subsections provide more detail on the development and implementation of the framework for OA and RPOs.

Open Access

OA remains poorly implemented, particularly at the distribution level.[14] SERCs have a critical role in putting in place the framework for OA, as they must notify OA regulations, establish an OA cross-subsidy surcharge to compensate the utility for the loss of paying consumers who choose an alternate supplier, determine wheeling and transmission charges, and notify a roadmap for the reduction of the OA cross-subsidy surcharge over time (and facilitate implementation).

Twenty-six SERCs have issued OA regulations, 24 have determined the OA surcharge, 22 the OA wheeling charge, and 25 the OA transmission charge (figure 4.6). Nineteen SERCs have issued the approach regulations and determined all the necessary charges for OA; of these 19, however, only 11 have also reduced the OA cross-subsidy surcharge since 2006 (13 SERCs in total have reduced the surcharge).

Beyond putting the structure for OA in place, SERCs also receive and approve OA applications. As of 2012, only 15 SERCs had received any OA applications. Of these, only 12 SERCs had approved any applications; and in only 10 states

Figure 4.6 Action Taken on OA by SERCs

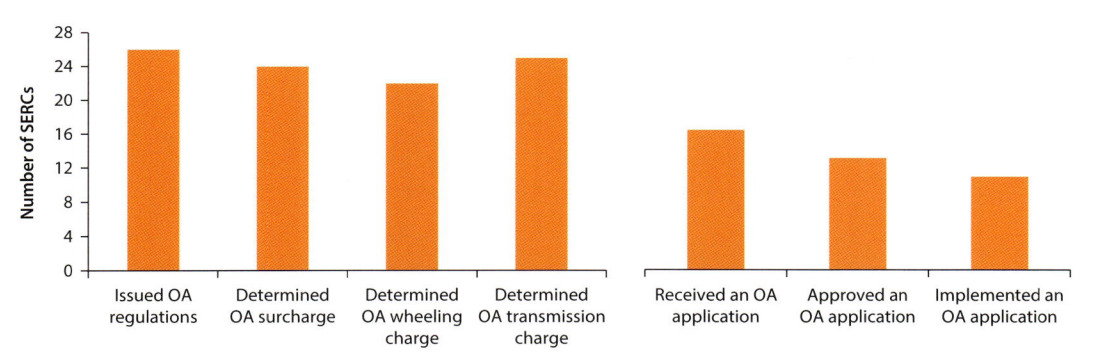

[Bar chart showing Number of SERCs on y-axis (0-28):
- Issued OA regulations: 26
- Determined OA surcharge: 24
- Determined OA wheeling charge: 22
- Determined OA transmission charge: 25
- Received an OA application: 17
- Approved an OA application: 14
- Implemented an OA application: 11]

Source: World Bank compilation.
Note: OA = open access; SERC = state electricity regulatory commission.

had any applications been implemented. The SERCs that have started receiving applications have received an average of 17, approved an average of 14, and seen an average of 11 implemented.

Renewable Energy and Energy Efficiency

Twenty-six SERCs have notified RPO regulations (figure 4.7); however, only 18 SERCs actually monitor compliance with the regulations, and only 4 SERCs issue penalties for noncompliance (Madhya Pradesh, Kerala, Jharkhand, and Haryana).

Five state regulators have defined RPO targets for the next five years (Andhra Pradesh, Delhi, Himachal Pradesh, Kerala, and West Bengal), but most SERCs (12) have only defined targets two years into the future. Compliance as of 2012 with solar RPO targets for 2012–13 varied widely: six states (Gujarat, Karnataka, Orissa, Punjab, Rajasthan, and Uttarakhand) had already met 100 percent of the target, but nine states had made no progress. On average, states had achieved about 44 percent of the target.

Twenty-one SERCs have established incentives for consumer DSM, though only 11 SERCs have issued regulations for energy efficiency and DSM. Measures taken include introducing a ToD tariff, directing utilities to develop programs to promote use of energy-efficient appliances, and conducting consumer awareness campaigns on energy efficiency and conservation.

Twenty-two SERCs have determined FITs for at least one type of renewable energy, but only 3 states have notified FITs for all the kinds of energy (other than solar) for which renewable potential exists (Delhi, Orissa, and Punjab). Another 5 states have notified FITs for 75–80 percent of the forms of energy for which they have potential (Gujarat, Kerala, Madhya Pradesh, Maharashtra, and Uttar Pradesh).[15] Twenty SERCs have issued ToD metering regulations, and 17 SERCs have provisions for a differential or ToD tariff. Twenty-four SERCs have notified renewable energy certificate regulations (that is, regulations that facilitate trading of such certificates).

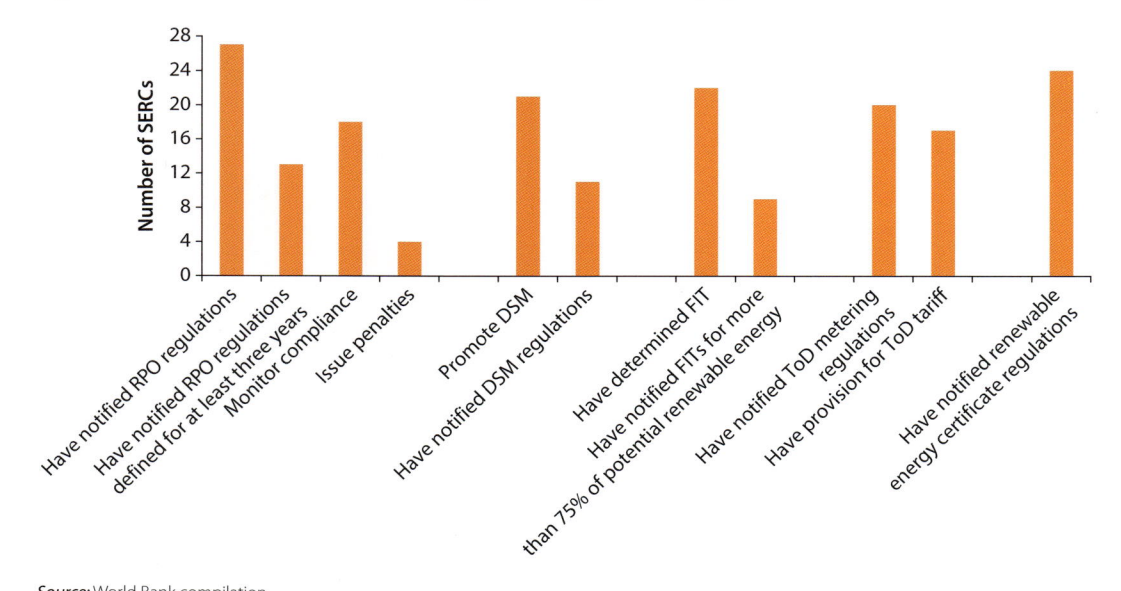

Figure 4.7 Action Taken on Renewable Energy and Energy Efficiency by SERCs

Category	Number of SERCs
Have notified RPO regulations	27
Have notified RPO regulations defined for at least three years	13
Monitor compliance	18
Issue penalties	4
Promote DSM	21
Have notified DSM regulations	11
Have determined FIT	22
Have notified FITs for more than 75% of potential renewable energy	9
Have notified ToD metering regulations	20
Have provision for ToD tariff	17
Have notified renewable energy certificate regulations	24

Source: World Bank compilation.
Note: DSM = demand-side management; FIT = feed-in-tariff; RPO = renewable purchase obligation; SERC = state electricity regulatory commission; ToD = time-of-day.

Institutional Design: SERC Autonomy, Capacity, Transparency, and Accountability

The review finds, first, that SERCs have struggled to achieve true autonomy from state governments, in part because of relationships built into the EA 2003. Second, many SERCs appear to lack the resources that might assist in performing their functions—most notably, enough professional staff and appropriate IT systems. Third, despite some major innovations in this area, most SERCs have yet to implement adequate transparency measures and create frameworks for meaningful public input to the regulatory process. Finally, perhaps most importantly, there is no clear accountability mechanism to govern SERCs themselves.

Autonomy

Many SERCs have struggled to achieve key benchmarks of autonomy: ensuring the SERC chairperson and other members complete full terms of five years (also key for instilling stability and predictability in the regulatory process), and obtaining assured funding that is not dependent on the vagaries of annual budget appropriations.

Financial Autonomy

Over half the SERCs still depend primarily on state grants for their budgets, and over 40 percent of the 23 SERCs with exact numbers available derive their entire budgets from the state (figure 4.8). One-quarter of SERCs depend mainly on their own revenue, and the rest are mixed commissions in Gujarat, Maharashtra,

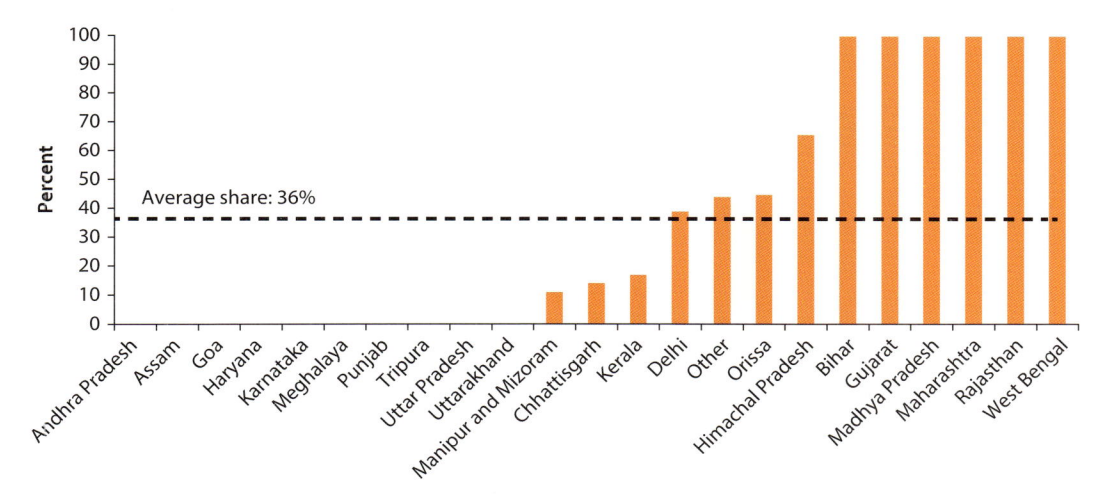

Figure 4.8 Share of SERC Budget from Own Resources

[Bar chart showing percent share of SERC budget from own resources by state. Average share: 36%. States with 0%: Andhra Pradesh, Assam, Goa, Haryana, Karnataka, Meghalaya, Punjab, Tripura, Uttar Pradesh, Uttarakhand. Manipur and Mizoram ~11%, Chhattisgarh ~14%, Kerala ~17%, Delhi ~39%, Other ~44%, Orissa ~45%, Himachal Pradesh ~65%, Bihar ~100%, Gujarat ~100%, Madhya Pradesh ~100%, Maharashtra ~100%, Rajasthan ~100%, West Bengal ~100%.]

Source: World Bank compilation.
Note: Five states, including Jharkhand and Tamil Nadu, did not have data on budget shares; Jharkhand State Electricity Regulatory Commission indicated that it funds itself from a mix of its own revenue and state grants, and the other four primarily from state grants.

Madhya Pradesh, Rajasthan, Bihar, and West Bengal stand out as the only SERCs that fund themselves entirely from their own revenues.

Financial autonomy often depends on the individual SERC's licensee base. Many of the SERCs that have achieved full financial autonomy, including MPERC, GERC, and MERC, have established comprehensive fee regulations with a detailed schedule of fees and charges levied for submission of petitions, requests for review of an order, renewal of annual license, and so on.[16] The success of these regulations in bringing in revenue probably stems from the states' high numbers of licensees, independent power producers, OA consumers, and high-value (generally industrial) consumers.

Member Tenure

Member tenure is an indication of SERC autonomy and is important for enhancing SERC effectiveness. Adequate tenure is necessary for a SERC member to understand the sector context and the states' utilities sufficiently to regulate the sector well. A short tenure may reflect tension between SERC members and the state government, possibly over government influence that can cause a SERC member to resign prematurely, or from the appointment of members less than five years before the mandatory retirement age of 65, which may occur when the state government appoints officials who are close to retirement or retirees from government service. In these ways, member tenure is indicative of the degree of influence the government exerts over the SERC.

The tenure of the chairperson and other members of the commission is typically five years, but actual tenure is much shorter in some states (figure 4.9). From 2000 to 2010 (or since the SERC was created), 16 states have had average chairperson tenures of under five years, and 8 have had less than the group

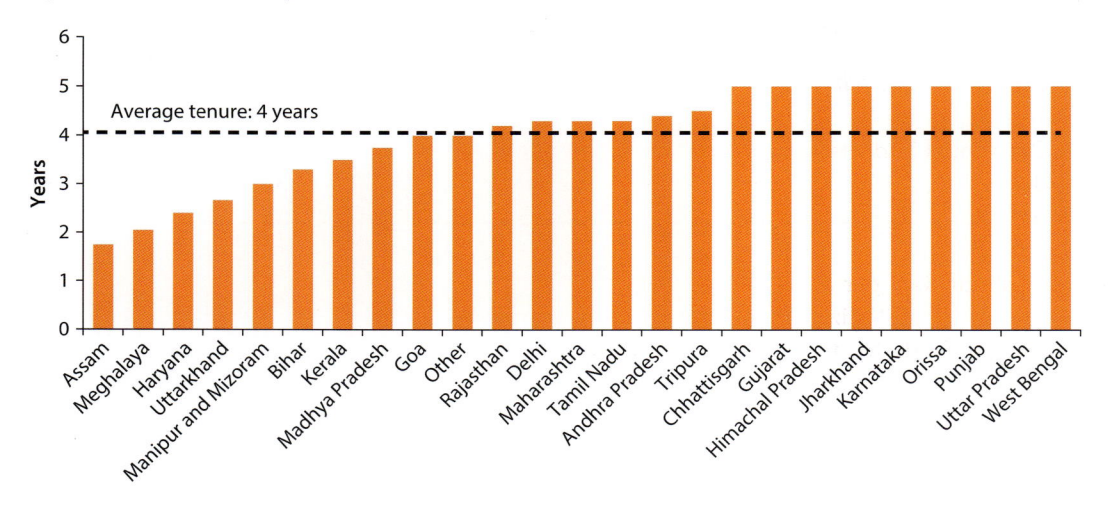

Figure 4.9 Tenure of Chairperson and Other Commission Members

[Bar chart showing tenure in years for various states, with an "Average tenure: 4 years" reference line. States from left to right: Assam (~1.75), Meghalaya (~2.0), Haryana (~2.4), Uttarkhand (~2.65), Manipur and Mizoram (3.0), Bihar (~3.3), Kerala (~3.5), Madhya Pradesh (~3.7), Goa (4.0), Other (4.0), Rajasthan (~4.2), Delhi (~4.3), Maharashtra (~4.3), Tamil Nadu (~4.3), Andhra Pradesh (~4.4), Tripura (~4.5), Chhattisgarh (5.0), Gujarat (5.0), Himachal Pradesh (5.0), Jharkhand (5.0), Karnataka (5.0), Orissa (5.0), Punjab (5.0), Uttar Pradesh (5.0), West Bengal (5.0).]

Source: World Bank compilation.

average of four years. Of the four SERCs supplying data on the tenure of other members, average tenures tended to be about the same as, or slightly longer than, average chairperson tenures.

Relationships Built into the EA 2003

Finally, built into the EA 2003 are clauses that seemingly contradict the principle of SERC autonomy. Most significantly, under section 108 the EA 2003 gives state governments the ability to provide binding "directions" to the SERCs in matters of policy involving the public interest, with the determination as to whether any specific direction is eligible being made by the state government itself. The Shunglu Committee report notes that some state governments have even issued directions to the regulator on specific aspects of tariff setting, including, in one case, to prevent it from issuing a tariff order.

The EA 2003 also gives state governments the power to select SERC members, with room for some subjectivity in these decisions. The pool of candidates for SERC positions is often the same as that for government and utility management positions; for example, outgoing state power secretaries are made SERC chairpersons on their retirement. Commissioners who have previously held positions of authority in government departments can find it difficult to exercise true independence from the government. The state government also generally approves the SERC's choices over the number, nature, and categories of SERC officers and other employees, and their remuneration.

As an instance of good practice, Gujarat has state legislation that specifies criteria for selecting SERC members. The Gujarat Electricity Industry (Reorganization and Regulation) Act of 2003 specifies that the two SERC members and chairperson must include one person with a background in engineering and electricity supply and two with experience in finance, industry, law, or management. In addition, all member appointees must be under 62 years of age to ensure they can serve at least three years before retirement.[17]

Commission Capacity
Budget
SERC annual budgets cover a wide range (from Rs 1 million in Tripura to Rs 96 million in Maharashtra). To compare budgets across SERCs, SERC budgets are normalized by the number of households with electricity access, a proxy for the size of the system the SERC must regulate. On this basis, SERC budgets range from about Rs 1 per household connection (Tripura and Kerala) through Rs 18 (the Manipur and Mizoram Joint Electricity Regulatory Commission [JERC] and Himachal Pradesh), to Rs 32 in the JERC for Goa and the union territories (figure 4.10). The median budget is about Rs 4.3 per household connection.

Staffing
Staffing levels and quality vary across SERCs, but all SERCs have difficulty attracting and retaining enough professional staff. SERCs average 38 staff in all but only 13 professional staff, less than the Forum of Regulators' recommended benchmark of 15 (figure 4.11). MERC exhibits by far the largest cadre of staff—50, of whom 40 are professional—which is commensurate with its scale of operations, including 10 licensees, one state generating company, and several independent power producers.

As SERCs offer limited career opportunities, they are generally restricted to hiring staff on a deputation or contract basis.[18] Relying on deputations (which requires permission from the releasing entity, usually another state government agency or even the utility itself) means SERC staffing numbers are under

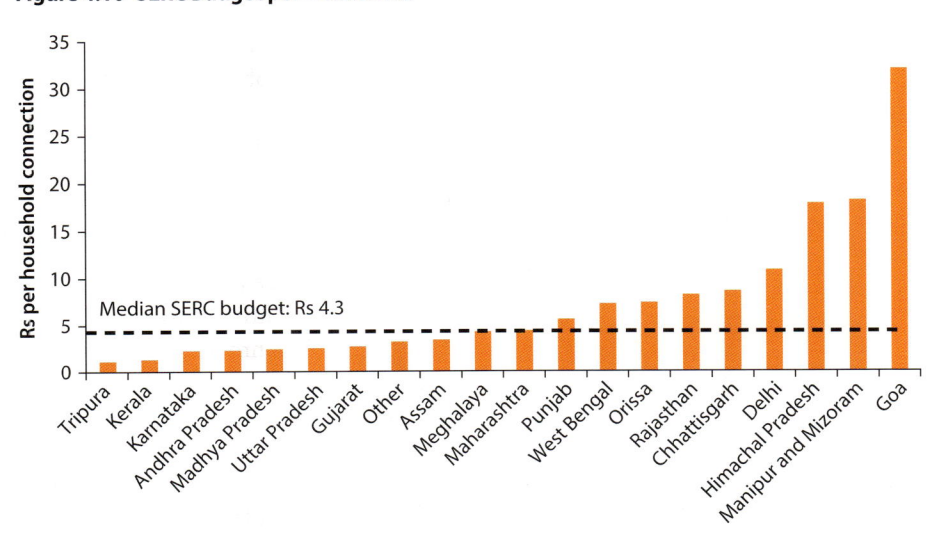

Figure 4.10 SERC Budget per Household

Source: World Bank compilation.
Note: SERC = state electricity regulatory commission.

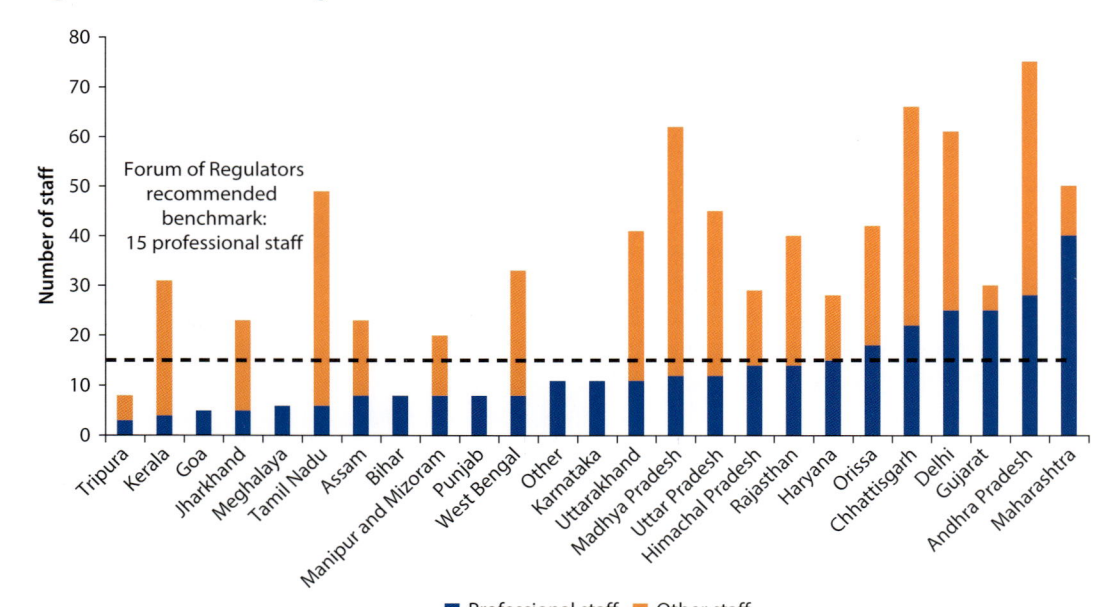

Figure 4.11 SERC Staff Strength

Forum of Regulators recommended benchmark: 15 professional staff

■ Professional staff ■ Other staff

Source: World Bank compilation.
Note: SERC = state electricity regulatory commission. SERCs that appear to have no "other staff" did not have data on number of nonprofessional staff. The figure shows full-time staff only and therefore excludes consultants.

government control; many governments have simply not provided adequate human resources to SERCs. For example, in Assam, the state government has not approved the hiring of new staff proposed by Assam Electricity Regulatory Commission over the past five years.

Some SERCs have addressed this challenge by relying heavily on long-term consultants, whose appointment does not require specific approval from the state government. For example, MPERC has contracted professional consultancy firms for tasks including training, capacity building (supported by the UK Department for International Development), drafting of regulations, and issuing tariff orders. In practice, few states have hired long-term consultants due to insufficient funding or lack of action to create appointments and set aside a budget. However, the use of consultants means that the commission does not build up the requisite expertise, "leaving a sense of disempowerment among staff, and a lack of institutional memory within the regulator."[19]

An exception to this pattern is MERC, which prefers to meet its requirement through direct recruitment rather than through deputation or by hiring consultants. This is helped by the presence of internal promotion avenues, which attracts more qualified candidates.

Information Management and IT

Few SERCs have installed Regulatory Information Management Systems (RIMS). Only 7 (of 26) SERCs report having one—Andhra Pradesh, Delhi, Gujarat,

Maharashtra, Orissa, Tamil Nadu, and Uttar Pradesh. SERCs can use a RIMS for compilation and analysis of data, including tariff norms, expense and revenue trends, and utilities' performance trajectories. Without RIMS, it is a challenge for a SERC to properly track utility performance (necessary for holding utilities accountable and providing appropriate incentives for future improvement), maintain adequate information for issuing MYTs, or even issue tariffs on time. SERCs without RIMS often collect data piecemeal from utilities, making data inconsistencies and collection delays more likely.

Transparency and Participatory Decision Making

Open public hearings with adequate notice, provision of information, including discussion papers, in the public domain, and "letting sunshine in on the process" of decision making are all critical to the legitimacy, and thus, ultimately, the power of the regulator, while also making the regulator accountable to its key constituencies, particularly consumers. Transparency also enables the regulator to hold both itself and its licensees to meeting the commitments it makes to consumers.

All but two SERCs (West Bengal and Sikkim) report holding public hearings before issuing a new tariff order, but only two-thirds of SERCs have updated hearing schedules on their websites, a critical tool for ensuring consumers can actually take advantage of the hearings (figure 4.12). In addition, the number, accessibility, and other qualities of hearings vary by state and can have a large impact on consumer participation (box 4.3). For example, GERC holds only a single two-to-three hour session and only publishes the notice of the hearing in one or two major daily papers, which may be why there is little public participation at

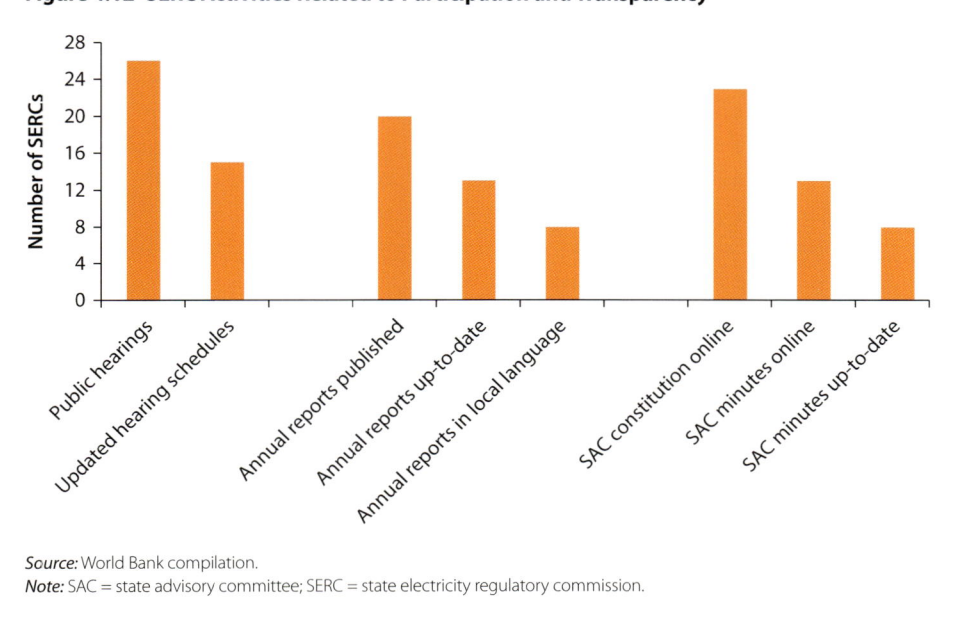

Figure 4.12 SERC Activities Related to Participation and Transparency

Source: World Bank compilation.
Note: SAC = state advisory committee; SERC = state electricity regulatory commission.

> **Box 4.3 Involving Consumers as Stakeholders: Selected SERC Experiences**
>
> Delhi Electricity Regulatory Commission (DERC) and Maharashtra Electricity Regulatory Commission (MERC) stand out as state electricity regulatory commissions (SERCs) that have developed innovative mechanisms to ensure public opinion is taken into account in regulatory proceedings, and Madhya Pradesh Electricity Regulatory Commission (MPERC) stands out for its efforts in increasing consumer awareness of standards of performance (SoP).
>
> DERC began conducting consumer surveys in 2007, and Delhi is the only state in which surveys are carried out regularly, with the results used to measure licensee performance. The survey asks 10,000–15,000 domestic consumers about their preferences along seven macro parameters (supply continuity, supply quality), their satisfaction with their distribution companies (discoms) along several micro parameters, and the relative importance to them of each one. Survey findings are published in DERC's annual reports, along with the scores of the three discoms and the best and worst performing areas of each discom.
>
> MERC is the only SERC to have formed a panel of Authorized Consumer Representatives to represent the interests of consumers in Commission proceedings. The panel also recommends capacity building for consumer groups, takes steps to improve the efficacy of the Commission's regulatory processes, educates consumers on demand-side management and on their service rights, and provides advice to the Commission on safeguarding consumers' interests in Commission orders and regulations.
>
> MPERC is one of the few SERCs that have taken significant steps to increase consumer awareness of SoP, a real challenge to successful implementation of these regulations. It monitors utilities' compliance with the standards and publishes an annual compliance report in newspapers, in English and Hindi, and on its website. It has also directed licensees to publish the SoP in key subdivision offices.

the hearings; only eight objections were received for the last petition. In contrast, DERC conducts three days of hearings, each lasting a full day and focusing on a different set of consumers, and publishes notices in seven daily papers. Likely in consequence, Delhi has seen a high degree of public participation: in 2012, 405 stakeholders submitted their objections to and comments on the tariff petition.

DERC issues news bulletins (in newspapers and other media) on topics such as calculation of aggregate technical and commercial (AT&C) losses, tariff determination, the need for additional capital expenditure, safety hazards in the installation of electrical equipment, and promotion of energy efficiency. It also issues press notes on key orders and decisions made, including changes in tariff design and rates, and it undertook a special drive for the redressal of consumer complaints. To ensure wider participation of stakeholders and the public, MPERC ensures publication of ARR petitions, draft regulations, minutes of public hearings, and other discussion papers through various media (in the local language and in English) and invites suggestions on these.

Most SERCs have websites (except Sikkim), though quality varies tremendously. Nagaland's does not work. All but two SERCs publish regulations online.[20]

Information about the functioning of the SAC is also published on the SERC website, including the list of members and the minutes of their meetings. Twenty-three SACs have their constitutions published online, but only 13 publish the minutes of their meetings online, and in only 8 are these up to date.

Twenty of the 26 SERCs providing data publish annual reports (online and often in other forums), though only one-third publish those reports in the local language. However, for 13 of the 20 SERCs that publish annual reports, the most recent is from 2011 or 2012; for the others, from 2008, 2009, or 2010. Their contents vary widely: for example, DERC and APERC's do not include important information about the functioning of the SERC, including any breakdown of Commission expenses, profile of key Commission staff, or training and capacity building by the Commission.

Accountability

All SERCs are technically accountable to the state legislature, in that prior to issuing rules or regulations they submit them for review to it. SERCs also file their audited accounts and annual reports with it. However, in practice, the state legislature rarely interferes with SERC functioning, asking few questions about rules and regulations, and rarely taking proactive steps. Even SERC budgets are usually passed with little debate.

An additional accountability channel is the Appellate Tribunal, established under the EA 2003 to hear appeals by those aggrieved by SERC orders and subjecting SERCs to judicial scrutiny. However, since the Tribunal is not mandated to routinely monitor or review SERC performance, its mandate would need to be modified for it to function as a proper mechanism for accountability.

The consumer protection measures that SERCs are required to put in place are an additional device for accountability. However, the lack of full public transparency and follow-through on noncompliance with SoP, as noted, constrains consumers' ability to hold SERCs accountable.

Likely in recognition of this, the Shunglu Committee recommended that steps be taken to monitor the performance of the SERCs and, in early 2013, the Government of India initiated discussion on a possible amendment to the EA 2003 to strengthen the framework of accountability for SERCs.

Indexes on Institutional Design and Implementation of Mandates

To organize the information under different heads and analyze the relative performance of SERCs, simple indexes (unweighted aggregates) were created (table 4.1).[21] Each index is composed of the components in the table, with the scoring noted. All SERCs (other than those in three small states, where data are very spotty) are included.[22] Appendixes F and G present the data points for the indexes as well as the scores for each SERC by subcomponent.

Two "overall" indexes were created as simple aggregates of these indexes to measure: aspects of Institutional Design (ID) together—that is, autonomy, transparency, and capacity of the regulator (in the absence of quantitative benchmarks,

Table 4.1 Indexes of SERC Institutional Design and Implementation of Regulatory Mandates

Index	Component	SERCs receive a 1 if…	Average score of all SERCs (%)
SERC institutional design (average score = 48.5%)			
Autonomy	• Average chairperson tenure over past 10 years • If budget is from own revenues or a mix of own revenues and state grants	>= 5 years Yes	42
Capacity	• RIMS • Number of professional staff	Yes >=15 (per Forum of Regulators recommendation)	28
Transparency	• Regulatory decisions online • Hold public hearings before tariff order • Updated hearing schedule online • Publish annual reports on website • Publish annual report in local language • SAC constitution online • SAC minutes online	Yes (1 point per item)	75
Implementation of regulatory mandates (average score = 74%)			
Tariffs	• From FY08 to FY10, number of years SERC published tariff order more than 120 days after receiving utilities' ARR filings • Share of years in existence (or years since FY01, whichever is less) in which SERC published a tariff order • 2010 average billed tariff equals or exceeds operating cost recovery level • Conducted cost of supply study • Issued MYT order	0 or 1 years > 66% Yes Yes Yes	47
Protection of consumer rights	• SERC has ombudsman • State advisory committee established • CGRF guidelines notified	Yes (1 point per item)	99
Standards of performance	• SERC has issued SoP regulations • Penalties for noncompliance clearly defined • SERC monitors compliance with standards • SERC issues penalties for noncompliance	Yes (1 point per item)	70
Other regulations	SERC has issued regulations on: • Supply code • Trading • Metering • MYT • Intrastate ABT	Yes (1 point per item)	71
Open access	• Issued OA regulations • Determined OA surcharge • Determined OA wheeling charge • Determined OA transmission charge • Received OA applications	Yes Yes Yes Yes Received >= 1	82
Renewable energy and energy efficiency	• Notified renewable energy regulations • RPOs are technology-specific • SERC monitors compliance with RPOs • SERC issues penalties for noncompliance • Determined an FIT • SERC has measures or incentives to promote consumer DSM • SERC has provision for ToD tariff • Issued energy efficiency/DSM regulations • Issued ToD metering regulations	Yes (1 point per item)	75

Source: World Bank compilation.

Note: ARR = annual revenue requirement; CGRF = consumer grievance-redressal forum; DSM = demand-side management; FIT = feed-in-tariff; MYT = multiyear tariff; OA = open access; RIMS = regulatory information management system; RPO = renewable purchase obligation; SAC = state advisory committee; SERC = state electricity regulatory commission; SoP = standards of performance; ToD = time-of-day.

an index could not be developed to measure regulator accountability); and implementation of key regulatory mandates (on tariffs, protection of consumers, SoP, OA, renewable energy, and notification of other regulations).[23]

The two indexes are significantly (at 1 percent) positively related with a correlation of 0.59, indicating that implementation of mandates (IM) moves in line with desirable ID (figure 4.13).

On ID, Gujarat, Orissa, Delhi, and Maharashtra are the highest-scoring SERCs overall (figure 4.14). Among the subcomponents the SERCs with the best scores are:

- *Autonomy:* Gujarat, Himachal Pradesh, Jharkhand, Orissa, and West Bengal.
- *Capacity:* Gujarat, Orissa, Maharashtra, Delhi, and Andhra Pradesh.
- *Transparency:* Gujarat, Delhi, and Maharashtra.

On IM, Andhra Pradesh, Himachal Pradesh, and Karnataka are the highest ranking (figure 4.15). By subcomponent:

- *Tariffs:* Delhi, Andhra Pradesh, Chhattisgarh, Himachal Pradesh, Karnataka, Kerala, Orissa, West Bengal, and Madhya Pradesh have the strongest scores (100 percent).
- *Consumer Protection:* All SERCs but one score 100 percent.
- *SoP:* Only Jharkhand scores 100 percent; many have 75 percent.

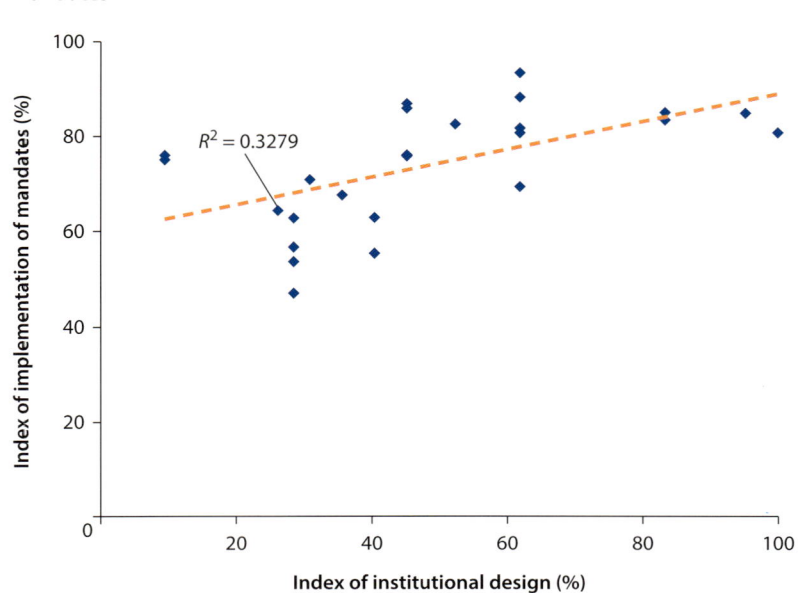

Figure 4.13 Index of Institutional Design vs. Index of Implementation of Mandates

[Scatter plot with $R^2 = 0.3279$; x-axis: Index of institutional design (%); y-axis: Index of implementation of mandates (%)]

Source: World Bank analysis.

Figure 4.14 Institutional Design Index Scores

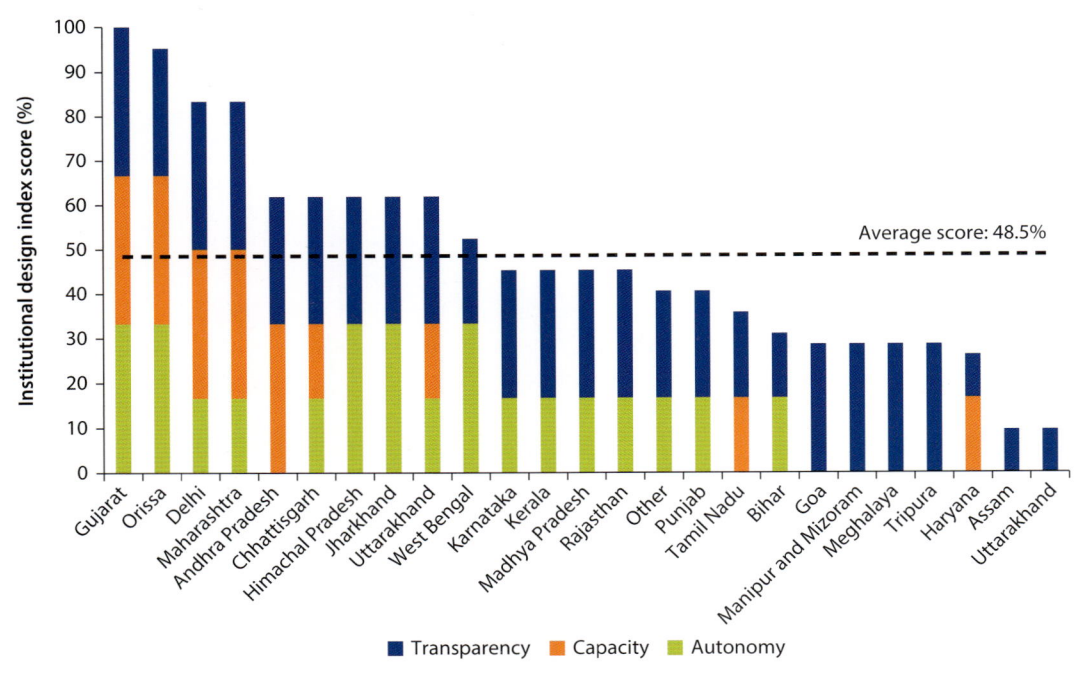

Average score: 48.5%

States (left to right): Gujarat, Orissa, Delhi, Maharashtra, Andhra Pradesh, Chhattisgarh, Himachal Pradesh, Jharkhand, Uttarakhand, West Bengal, Karnataka, Kerala, Madhya Pradesh, Rajasthan, Other, Punjab, Tamil Nadu, Bihar, Goa, Manipur and Mizoram, Meghalaya, Tripura, Haryana, Assam, Uttarakhand

Legend: Transparency, Capacity, Autonomy

Source: World Bank compilation.

Figure 4.15 Implementation of Mandates Index Scores

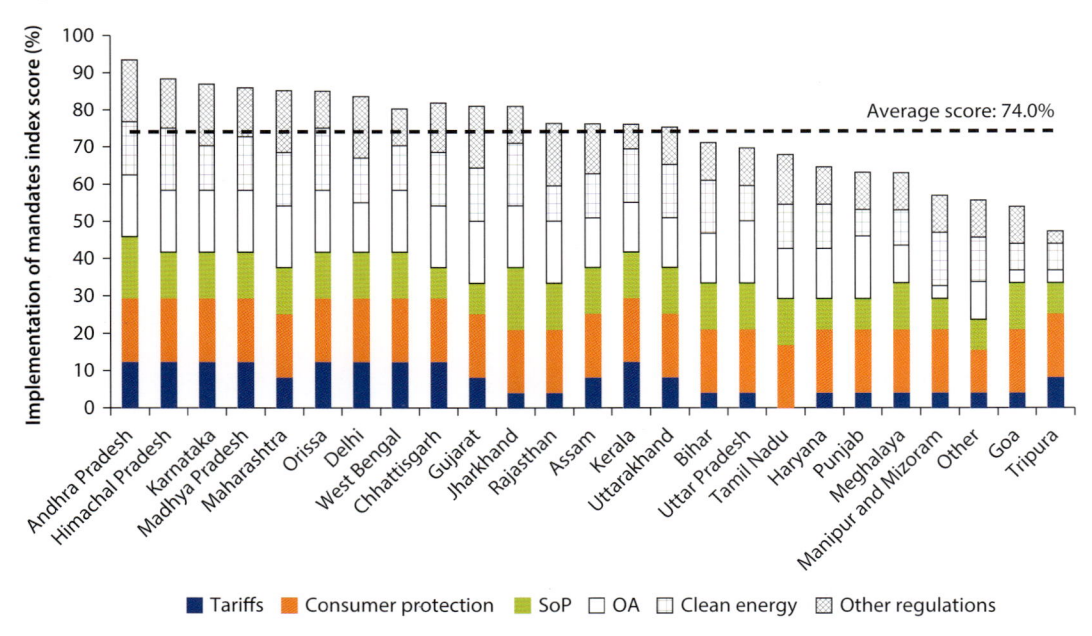

Average score: 74.0%

States (left to right): Andhra Pradesh, Himachal Pradesh, Karnataka, Madhya Pradesh, Maharashtra, Orissa, Delhi, West Bengal, Chhattisgarh, Gujarat, Jharkhand, Rajasthan, Assam, Kerala, Uttarakhand, Bihar, Uttar Pradesh, Tamil Nadu, Haryana, Punjab, Meghalaya, Manipur and Mizoram, Other, Goa, Tripura

Legend: Tariffs, Consumer protection, SoP, OA, Clean energy, Other regulations

Source: World Bank compilation.
Note: OA = open access; SoP = standards of performance.

Governance of Indian State Power Utilities • http://dx.doi.org/10.1596/978-1-4648-0303-1

- *OA:* Andhra Pradesh, Chhattisgarh, Himachal Pradesh, Karnataka, Madhya Pradesh, Gujarat, Orissa, Maharashtra, Jharkhand, West Bengal, Rajasthan, Uttar Pradesh, and Punjab all score 100 percent.
- *Clean Energy:* Himachal Pradesh, Orissa, and Jharkhand have the strongest scores (100 percent).
- *Other Regulations:* Andhra Pradesh, Gujarat, Maharashtra, Karnataka, Delhi, and Rajasthan have the top scores (100 percent).

Consistent with intuition, the length of time the SERC has been in existence ("SERC years") is significantly correlated with the capacity of the regulator as well as with the aggregate ID index (table 4.2). The average SERC score on ID is 48.5 percent.

On IM, the subindex on OA is correlated with several of the other subindexes—SERCs that are active on OA are likely to be active in other areas as well (table 4.3). The subindexes on consumer protection and SoP tend not to be correlated with the other subindexes. Thus there appears to be considerable variation across SERCs in areas of activity—a SERC that is active on one topic may do very little on others. Again, the length of time the SERC has been

Table 4.2 Correlation among Components of Institutional Design Index

	SERC years	Overall institutional design	Autonomy	Capacity	Transparency
SERC years	1				
Overall institutional design	0.4869**	1			
Autonomy	0.3264	0.7231***	1		
Capacity	0.5527***	0.7524***	0.1771	1	
Transparency	0.0143	0.6548***	0.3356*	0.3149	1

Source: World Bank analysis.
Note: SERC = state electricity regulatory commission.
Significance level: * = 10 percent, ** = 5 percent, *** = 1 percent.

Table 4.3 Correlation among Components of Implementation of Mandates Index

	SERC years	Overall implementation of mandates	Tariffs	Consumer protection	Other regulations	SoP	OA	Clean energy
SERC years	1							
Overall implementation of mandates	0.6592***	1						
Tariffs	0.4012**	0.70***	1					
Consumer protection	0.5246***	0.29	0.18	1				
Other regulations	0.4360**	0.67***	0.25	0.11	1			
SoP	0.2321	0.59***	0.22	0.27	0.28	1		
OA	0.7212***	0.83***	0.40**	0.14	0.53***	0.42**	1	
Clean Energy	0.1843	0.60***	0.39*	0.05	0.24	0.27	0.34*	1

Source: World Bank analysis.
Note: OA = open access; SERC = state electricity regulatory commission; SoP = standards of performance.
Significance level: * = 10 percent, ** = 5 percent, *** = 1 percent.

in existence is significantly correlated with the IM. The average SERC score on IM is 74 percent.

Since 2012, the Independent Power Producers Association of India has produced a ranking of regulators that includes elements of ID as well as implementation performance. It covers regulatory assets as a share of ARR and cost-recovery ratio for the utilities regulated, notification of various regulations (OA, RPOs, SoP), the average delay in issuance of tariff orders, and frequency of tariff revisions. An independent jury selects an award winner each year based on the ranking of SERCs along these parameters and an assessment of performance on aspects such as initiatives to combat power shortages, introduction of innovative mechanisms for cost recovery, introduction of ToD tariffs, diversity in professional origin of SERC members, independence shown in tariff setting (including through setting FITs and preferential tariffs), and how much the regulator monitors compliance with its directives. In 2012, the award was given to the Andhra Pradesh Electricity Regulatory Commission and in 2013 to the Kerala Electricity Regulatory Commission.

Notes

1. "Regulation of electricity industry is not new in India. But new regulatory arrangements for the industry are different in two important ways. First, the relevant Acts of 1998 and 2003 reduce direct control of the industry, and second, regulatory bodies have definite objectives that are not linked to electoral politics" (Kodwani 2009, 7).
2. Prior to the establishment of separate electricity regulators, the government fixed tariffs for state electricity boards.
3. Although the context of Berg's work is water, the issues arising from state ownership of utilities are also relevant to power.
4. The tariff considered in this analysis is the average billed tariff, defined as revenue billed divided by energy billed (that is, sold).
5. Clearly this tariff level would exceed average cost. With this tariff, however, the utility would make a profit as long as it had less than 10 percent distribution losses even as it maintained 100 percent collection.
6. In the remaining two states, if utilities had sold all the energy they purchased, their revenues would have covered their costs, but if they had lost even 10 percent of energy purchased (such as through technical distribution losses), thus not billing for that energy, their revenues would not have covered their costs.
7. Issuing a tariff order does not mean that tariffs were revised.
8. For SERCs created since 2001, we consider the percent of years for which the SERC was in existence that it issued a tariff order.
9. Regulatory assets are dues to the discoms, typically on account of tariff increases that the regulator accepts as justified but does not allow the discom to pass through to customers via the tariff in the year they are incurred. This is done to avoid a sudden jump in tariffs on the presumption that the dues will be recovered through gradual tariff increases in the future.
10. Unsuccessful challenges have included cases in which the appeal lacked legal ground (for example, some appeals reflect general consumer resistance to tariff hikes).

11. Meghalaya had one of the largest percentage increases of all states in the ratio of average billed tariff to operating-cost-recovery level during 2008–10. Two other states (Punjab and West Bengal) improved cost recovery somewhat, and the remaining three states actually saw a drop in cost recovery despite frequent tariff increases.
12. Cost of supply studies are usually carried out by independent agencies and cover a particular year. They are updated (rather than redone) in subsequent years.
13. For example, performance standards would include penalties for not restoring supply soon enough following a distribution transformer failure. One SERC's standard is for supply to be restored within 24 hours of such a failure in an urban area; failing this, utilities must pay each affected consumer Rs 100 per day of delay up to a maximum of Rs 3,000 per consumer.
14. The Electricity Act of 2003 defines open access as "nondiscriminatory provision for the use of transmission lines or distribution system or associated facilities with such lines or system by any licensee or consumer or a person engaged in generation."
15. Data obtained from the Ministry of New and Renewable Energy.
16. These fees are deposited in the SERC Fund (which states are required to establish). The SERC Fund enables easier accounting of funds used for the SERC and increases the transparency of SERC funding. Only eight states have established these funds: Assam, Chhattisgarh, Himachal Pradesh, Jharkhand, Madhya Pradesh, Nagaland, Orissa, and Uttar Pradesh.
17. GERC's chairperson is a retired IAS officer with experience in field organization and policy making, including for the power sector; one member is an electrical engineer with 34 years of experience in the Central Electricity Authority; and the other has an MBA in finance, a PhD in management, and 30 years of experience with Gujarat's electricity utilities.
18. Partly due to the fact that pay scales and benefits are in line with government norms, SERCs cannot easily attract qualified personnel from the private sector. In addition, most SERCs are small and have few avenues for promotion of staff within the organization, which makes them less attractive to public sector personnel as well.
19. J. L. Bajaj, former chairperson, Uttar Pradesh Electricity Regulatory Commission, 2012, private communication.
20. SERC websites also commonly include names and contact information for the chair and members, organization charts, utility average revenue requirement filings, tariff orders, other orders (such as dispute resolution orders, tariffs for renewable energy sources), schedules of tariff and other hearings, annual accounts, and contact information for utility CGRFs and SERC ombudsmen. Better websites include greater detail on each (such as profiles of SERC members, information about past SERC members), archives of past annual reports and other publications, and right to information and other key documents. Lower quality websites often lack updated annual accounts or audits, updated hearing schedules, key contact details, organization charts, and other basic information.
21. The benchmarks in table 4.1 are taken from legislation or recommended practices, apart from standards for publishing tariff orders annually and on time, which are as specified in the table.
22. The exclusion of these three states may skew average scores upward, as they had generally not achieved the benchmarks considered in this review for which data were available.

23. Other papers focusing on regulatory governance have followed similar strategies for benchmarking regulators; see Andres and others (2007), for example. Similarly, the Electricity Governance Initiative has created a toolkit for assessing regulators, benchmarking best practice, and promoting accountability among electricity governance bodies; see Dixit and others (2007).

References

Andres, Luis, Jose L. Guasch, Makhtar Diop, and Sebastian L. Azumendi. 2007. "Assessing the Governance of Electricity Regulatory Agencies in the Latin American and Caribbean Region: A Benchmarking Analysis." Policy Research Working Paper 4380, World Bank, Washington, DC.

Berg, Sanford V. 2013. *Best Practices in Regulating State-Owned and Municipal Water Utilities*. ECLAC Project Document. Santiago: Economic Commission for Latin America and the Caribbean.

Dixit, Shantanu, Navroz K. Dubash, Crescencia Maurer, and Smita Nakhooda. 2007. "Benchmarking Best Practice and Promoting Accountability in the Electricity Sector." The Electricity Governance Initiative, World Resources Institute, Washington, DC.

ICRA. 2012. *State-Owned Electricity Distribution Companies: Some Positives, Though Several Concerns Remain*. New Delhi: ICRA Limited.

Kodwani, Devendra. 2009. "Regulatory Institution and Regulatory Practice: Issues in Electricity Tariff Determination in Reformed Electricity Industry in India." http://papers.ssrn.com/sol3/papers.cfm?abstract_id=1517180.

Lal, Sumir. 2006. "Can Good Economics Ever Be Good Politics? Case Study of India's Power Sector." Working Paper 83, World Bank, Washington, DC.

Nair, Viraj. 2013. "Discoms Weighed Down by Rs 70,000-Crore Dues." *The Indian Express*, June 24.

Prayas Energy Group. 2003. *A Good Beginning but Challenges Galore: A Survey Based Study of Resources, Transparency, and Public Participation in Electricity Regulatory Commissions in India*. Prayas Occasional Report –1/2003. Pune, India.

Sethi, Aman. 2013. "The Price of Power." *The Hindu* (accessed October 28, 2013), http://www.hindu.com.

Stern, Jon, and Stuart Holder. 1999. "Regulatory Governance: Criteria for Assessing the Performance of Regulatory Systems—An Application to Infrastructure Industries in the Developing Countries of Asia." *Utilities Policy* 8 (1): 33–50.

CHAPTER 5

Relationships between Governance and Utility Performance

This chapter examines the links between specific corporate governance (CG) practices and utility performance, as well as the link between state electricity regulatory commission (SERC) design (indexes of capacity, autonomy, and transparency) and implementation of mandates (IM), both key elements of regulatory governance, and utility performance.

Utility performance is measured by three separate variables—profit after tax (PAT)[1] per unit of power,[2] PAT per unit of power net of subsidies booked,[3] and aggregate technical and commercial (AT&C) losses (which is applicable only to distribution utilities). The analysis looks separately at the set of all utilities for which financial performance data were available,[4] and at the set of utilities for which CG data were obtained in addition to the financial performance data. There are too few distribution companies (discoms), generation companies (gencos), and transmission companies (transcos) in the dataset to perform robust disaggregated analysis by group, although correlations among only discoms are reported below. As noted earlier, the governance data collected are for 2010 only, so this is a cross-section analysis. Summary statistics are in table 5.1.

International and India-specific recommendations on CG consistently emphasize the importance of a core set of CG structures and practices, such that the expected relationship between utility performance and the governance variables is as follows:

- A higher share of independent directors will be associated with stronger performance.
- Unclear relationship between share of executive directors and performance, though the fact that the Department of Public Enterprises restricts the share would indicate a negative expected relationship.[5]
- Chairman and managing director tenure is expected to be positively related to firm performance since it not only means stability in direction and ability to

Table 5.1 Summary Statistics

		Unit	Number of observations	Minimum	Maximum	Mean	Standard deviation
Measures of utility performance	AT&C loss rate (2011)	%	53	7.20	72.86	30.91	14.79
	AT&C loss rate (2010)	%	53	7.76	70.44	31.28	13.54
	Profit/Unit without subsidy (2011)	Rs/kWh	84	−4.50	0.44	−0.61	1.01
	Profit/Unit without subsidy (2010)	Rs/kWh	83	−4.03	0.60	−0.63	0.98
	Profit/Unit without subsidy (discoms only, 2011)	Rs/kWh	53	−4.50	0.35	−0.99	1.11
	Profit/Unit without subsidy (discoms only, 2010)	Rs/kWh	53	−4.03	0.38	−0.96	1.02
	Profit/Unit with subsidy (discoms only, 2011)	Rs/kWh	53	−4.50	0.35	−0.56	1.05
	Profit/Unit with subsidy (discoms only, 2010)	Rs/kWh	53	−4.03	0.38	−0.50	0.85
State-level variables	GDP per capita (2010)	Rs	29	16,119.42	132,715.90	50,477.64	25,686.33
	GDP per capita (2009)	Rs	29	13,980.14	119,272.5	44,340.71	22,600.76
	Holding company/bundled dummy	Categorical	29	0.00	1.00	0.66	0.48
Utility-level variables	Discom dummy[a]	Categorical	85	0.00	1.00	0.62	0.49
	Profit/Unit without subsidy (2007)	Rs/kWh	84	−5.68	3.08	−0.34	0.92
	Net fixed assets (2010)	Rs Crore	82	250.00	167,194.80	26,801.22	28,887.07
	Net fixed assets (2009)	Rs Crore	82	10.00	150,915.30	24,080.65	25,083.49
Corporate governance variables (2010)	Number of directors	Number	68	4.00	15.00	8.15	2.35
	Average CMD tenure	Years	41	0.80	5.00	2.24	1.05
	Basic CG index[b]	Number	66	0.38	1.00	0.65	0.16
	Detailed CG index	Number	21	0.22	0.89	0.49	0.20
	% of board that is independent directors	%	67	0.00	0.57	0.15	0.16
	% of board that is executive directors	%	67	0.00	0.83	0.35	0.22
	% of board that is government directors	%	67	0.17	1.00	0.48	0.22
Regulatory governance variables (2010)	ID index	Number	26	0.10	1.00	0.48	0.24
	IM index	Number	26	0.47	0.93	0.74	0.13

Source: World Bank compilation.

Note: AT&C = aggregate technical and commercial; CG = corporate governance; CMD = chairman and managing director; ID = institutional design; IM = implementation of mandates. a. For this analysis, we use "discom" to refer to any utility directly serving consumers (the same distinction made by the Power Finance Corporation when reporting data by utility type). Thus "discoms" includes distribution companies, state electricity boards, power departments, and bundled corporations.
b. The Basic CG index is the mean of compliance (0,1) with the following: having independent directors represent at least 33 percent of board strength (or 50 percent if the chair is an executive director); having two or fewer government directors; having executive directors represent no more than 50 percent of board strength; board size less than or equal to 12; having an audit committee; using an external auditor; publicly publishing audits; and publicly publishing annual accounts. See Chapter 3 for more detail.

conceive and implement strategic change but also is an indicator of the absence of state interference in the utility.
- Board size is expected to be negatively related to performance (since larger boards are less likely to be efficient or focused in their decision making) or might have an inverted U-shaped relationship with performance, with a "mid-size" board being optimal.
- As the broad "basic" CG index reflects an aggregation of "recommended practices," it is expected to be positively related to performance.
- The two indexes of regulatory governance (institutional design [ID] and implementation of mandates [IM]) are expected to be positively related to utility performance.

The following sections present Pearson correlations between the measures of performance and (a) the variables measuring aspects of CG and (b) regulatory governance. This is followed by exploratory regression analysis in which variations in performance are related to these factors, controlling for basic characteristics of the utilities and aspects of the environment they operate in.

Corporate Governance

The basic CG index is not correlated with either measure of profit (table 5.2). The relatively tight distribution around a high mean score indicates that there is generally high compliance with the recommendations on CG by utilities.

On the other hand, the detailed index is strongly positively correlated (significant at the 1 percent level) with profit excluding subsidies for all utilities and for discoms only (table 5.2; figure 5.1). This index only covers 20 utilities,[6] making the significance of these results all the more striking. The observed correlation is consistent with the idea that the more demanding implementation-related aspects of CG captured in the detailed index strongly affect company performance. The basic index focuses on board size and structure, which may be somewhat superficial—the real impact on performance depends on more meaningful attributes of processes and management within the organization. Higher-quality boards are likely to induce internal organizational and process changes in response to their demands for better information and their interest in holding management accountable for delivery of results. It is this that creates the pressure to perform better in the institution. This reasoning is consistent with the idea that measures of CG practices should go beyond simply ticking boxes and for boards to be strategic and demanding when fulfilling their mandates.

Another explanation consistent with the observed lack of correlation between the basic index and utility profits comes from the evidence—much of it qualitative—that the state government remains a big presence in these utilities and has a say in critical decisions, despite the formal creation of a board to insulate management from state interference. This means the state as owner can undermine the board, so the fact that the board structure and size are consistent

Table 5.2 Correlation between Corporate Governance Variables and Performance

		Number of directors	CMD tenure	Basic CG index	Detailed CG index	% of board that is independent directors	% of board that is executive directors	% of board that is government directors
Performance variables	State GDP per capita, 2010	0.050	0.122	−0.051	0.254	0.007	0.043	−0.080
	Profit/Unit without subsidy (2011)	0.066	0.220	0.039	0.621***	0.170	−0.222*	0.016
	Profit/Unit without subsidy (2010)	0.104	0.370**	0.072	0.621***	0.258***	−0.220*	−0.060
	Profit/Unit without subsidy (discom only, 2011)	0.067	0.285	−0.068	0.751***	0.149	−0.358**	0.024
	Profit/Unit without subsidy (discom only, 2010)	0.086	0.523**	−0.059	0.791***	0.238	−0.406**	−0.502
	Profit/Unit with subsidy (discom only, 2011)	0.339**	−0.202	0.052	0.507*	−0.025	−0.297*	0.191
	Profit/Unit with subsidy (discom only, 2010)	0.456***	0.166	−0.090	0.612*	−0.124	−0.210	0.124
	AT&C loss rate, 2011	−0.059	−0.143	−0.216	−0.314	−0.131	−0.311*	0.206
	AT&C loss rate, 2010	−0.066	−0.134	−0.159	−0.117	−0.058	−0.397**	0.262

Source: World Bank analysis.

Note: AT&C = aggregate technical and commercial; CG = corporate governance; CMD = chairman and managing director; GDP = gross domestic product. CMD Tenure row only shows correlation for the 41 firms for which data on CMD tenure are available; Detailed CG index row only shows correlation for the 20 firms that it covers and that have performance data.
Significance level: * = 10 percent, ** = 5 percent, *** = 1 percent.

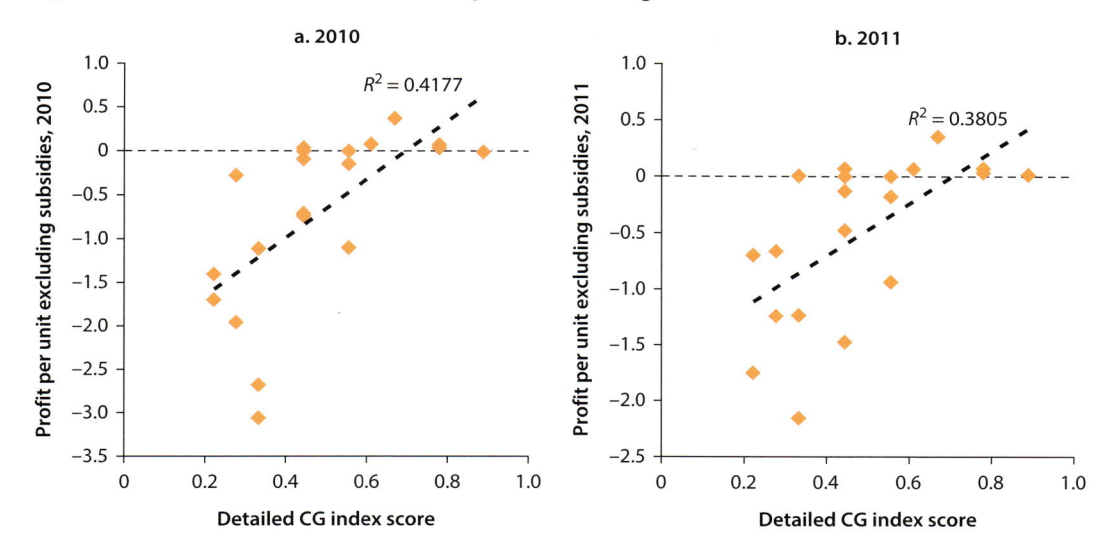

Figure 5.1 Detailed CG Index Score vs. Profit per Unit Excluding Subsidies

a. 2010 — $R^2 = 0.4177$

b. 2011 — $R^2 = 0.3805$

Source: World Bank analysis.
Note: CG = corporate governance; R^2 = coefficient of determination. Profit per unit is measured in Rs/kWh.

with recommended practices or statutory requirements would not necessarily be associated with better performance.

The correlation between the indexes of CG and state gross domestic product per capita is not significant; this is somewhat surprising since demand for good governance is generally felt to increase with the level of development. All else equal, one would expect quality of governance to be higher in higher income jurisdictions. The correlation with AT&C loss rate is also not significant.

Regulatory Governance

Correlations between the two aggregate regulatory governance indexes (ID and IM) and measures of utility performance are in table 5.3. The level of observation is the utility, not the SERC, as performance is at the utility level.

The ID index is highly positively correlated with utility profits, measured across all utilities and for the discom-only sample. The autonomy and capacity subindexes are also highly correlated with profitability. One inference is that these features of the regulatory commission are important indicators of the quality of the regulatory framework in the state, which is a critical determinant of the operating environment and thus performance of the utilities. The correlation with AT&C losses is not significantly different from zero, possibly because the latter is almost completely under the control of the utility and not affected by regulatory actions.

The index measuring the implementation of regulatory mandates is significantly correlated with profit per unit net of subsidies, as are the tariff and

Table 5.3 Correlation between Regulatory Governance Indexes and Utility Performance

	State GDP per capita (2010)	Profit/Unit without subsidy (2011)	Profit/Unit without subsidy (2010)	Profit/Unit without subsidy (2011)	Profit/Unit without subsidy (2010)	Discoms only			
						Profit/Unit with subsidy (2011)	Profit/Unit with subsidy (2010)	AT&C losses (2011)	AT&C losses (2010)
ID index	0.136	**0.398***	**0.365***	**0.532***	**0.471***	**0.429***	**0.397***	−0.138	−0.143
Autonomy	−0.174	**0.315***	**0.246***	**0.411***	**0.349***	**0.328****	**0.276***	0.078	0.051
Capacity	0.315	**0.383***	**0.392***	**0.453***	**0.400***	**0.381***	**0.338***	−0.221	−0.216
Transparency	0.162	0.114	0.089	**0.244***	**0.249***	0.168	**0.242***	−0.164	−0.149
IM index	−0.051	**0.412***	**0.327***	**0.484***	**0.360****	**0.607***	**0.534***	**−0.367***	**−0.305***
Tariffs	0.030	**0.454***	**0.482***	**0.559***	**0.548***	**0.448***	**0.469***	**−0.292***	−0.177
Consumer protection	0.149	0.064	0.109	0.186	0.175	**0.292***	**0.306***	**−0.449***	**−0.45***
Other regulations	0.213	0.159	0.041	0.179	0.066	**0.440***	**0.410***	**−0.562***	**−0.38***
SoP	0.002	0.091	0.043	0.154	0.087	**0.337****	**0.304****	−0.087	**−0.267***
OA	−0.177	**0.395***	**0.199***	**0.428***	0.209	**0.672***	**0.488***	−0.162	−0.128
Clean energy	−0.281	0.175	**0.221***	0.182	0.190	−0.009	−0.030	0.048	0.000

Source: World Bank analysis.

Note: Discom = distribution company; GDP = gross domestic product; AT&C = aggregate technical and commercial; ID = institutional design; IM = implementation of mandates; R^2 = coefficient of determination SoP = standards of performance; OA = open access. The bold values are of the two regulatory indexes, and the non-bolded values are the components of each index.
Significance level: * = 10 percent, ** = 5 percent, *** = 1 percent.

Figure 5.2 Institutional Design Index and Implementation of Mandates Index vs. Profit per Unit Including Subsidies

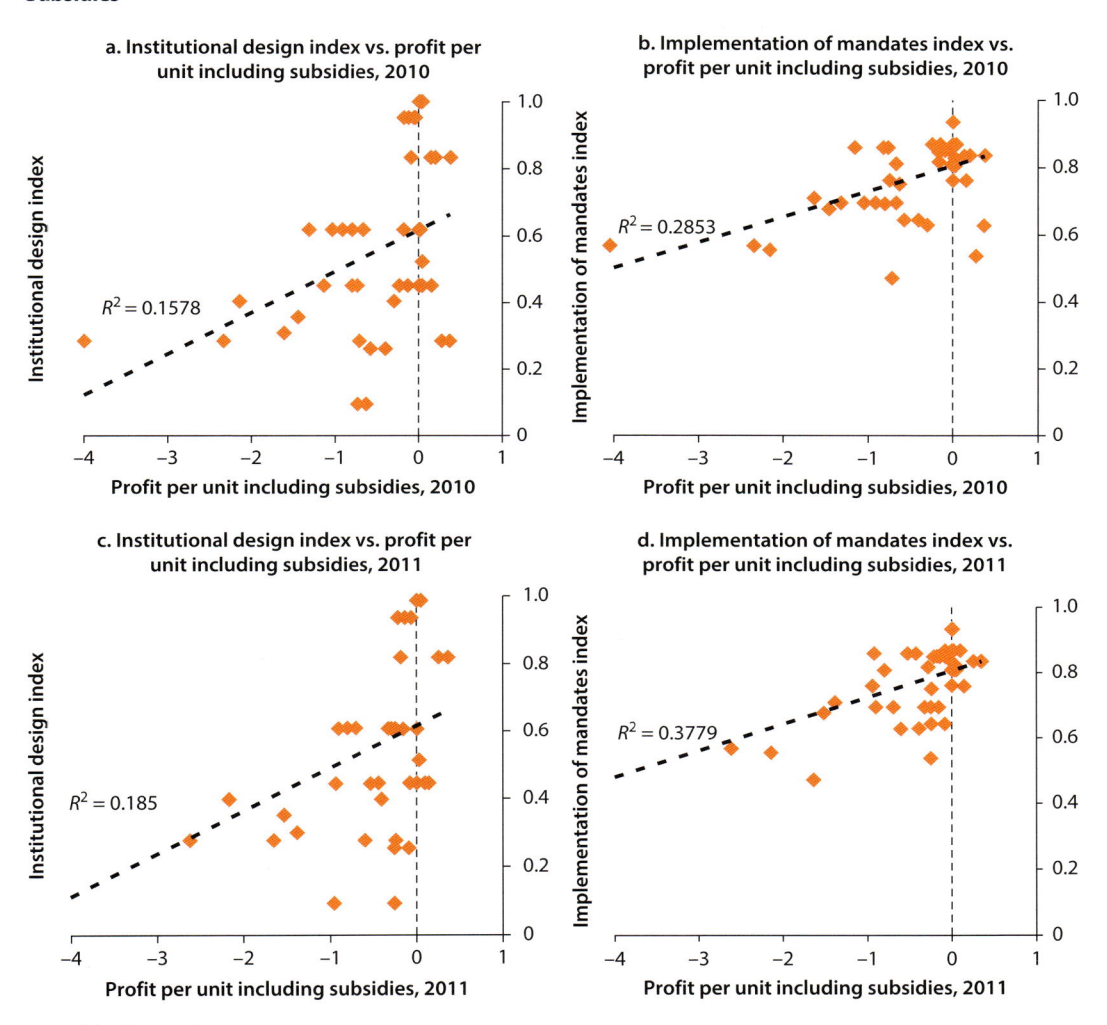

a. Institutional design index vs. profit per unit including subsidies, 2010 — $R^2 = 0.1578$

b. Implementation of mandates index vs. profit per unit including subsidies, 2010 — $R^2 = 0.2853$

c. Institutional design index vs. profit per unit including subsidies, 2011 — $R^2 = 0.185$

d. Implementation of mandates index vs. profit per unit including subsidies, 2011 — $R^2 = 0.3779$

Source: World Bank analysis.
Note: Distribution companies only; R^2 = coefficient of determination. Profit per unit is measured in Rs/kWh.

open access (OA) subindexes (figure 5.2). However, the IM index and subindexes other than clean energy have a greater (positive) correlation with profit/unit including subsidies and a significant negative correlation with AT&C loss levels—both as one might intuitively expect. The latter are both measures of discom performance and the regulatory mandates, particularly protection of consumer rights, tariffs, standards of performance, and OA, are particularly applicable to discoms. This may therefore be a reflection of the strength of the link between the functioning of the regulator and utility performance.

Governance and Performance

This section reports on the results of an exploratory analysis of the relationship between utility performance and governance structures and practices, controlling for other factors that are expected to affect performance. Ordinary least squares regressions are used to test the following stylized model of the determinants of utility performance:

$$Utility\ Performance_{ij} = \alpha + \beta_1 CG_i + \beta_2 UTIL_i + \beta_3 REG_j + \beta_4 STATE_j + \varepsilon_{ij}$$

for utility i in state j, where CG denotes corporate governance, REG denotes regulatory governance, $UTIL$ is a set of utility-specific controls, $STATE$ is a set of state-level controls, and ε is a random error term assumed to follow a standard normal distribution.

Utility performance, controlling for utility specific structural features, is expected to be affected by the utility's external operating environment, which includes factors such as state characteristics and the regulator and its actions, as well as internal accountability factors that affect the efficiency of the utility's own operations.

Utility size (proxied by the log of net fixed assets from the previous year), profit per unit for 2007, and a dummy for whether the utility performs distribution functions are the three utility controls used in the analysis. The first is included to capture scale effects and the second to control for starting values that are likely to act as a drag on current performance. The discom dummy is included to control for the significant difference in performance of discoms and all other types of utilities. State per capita income of the year before is used as an indicator of level of development, general capacity, and expectations of good service which might be expected to translate into higher performing utilities. Finally, the regulatory governance indexes measuring institutional development (ID) and degree of implementation of mandates (IM) are included as controls for the institutional quality and functioning of the regulator.

Tables 5.4 and 5.5 present the results of this regression, which are consistent with intuition in many respects: state gross domestic product per capita is strongly positively related to performance; profits per unit are positively related to per unit profits in 2007 and are significantly lower for discoms. Discoms are well known to have higher losses than the upstream businesses of generation and transmission that are subject to cost-plus regulation or can pass through their costs. However, there appear to be diseconomies of scale, with larger utilities (measured by net fixed assets) generally being less profitable, although the result is not consistently significant.

The coefficients on the regulatory governance index ID are significantly positively related to profit per unit, as expected. As noted above, the ID index captures the features of the regulatory framework, including predictability, certainty, and quality of regulatory decisions that are expected to impact utility strategic and operational choices, while the IM index goes to the heart of how active the

Table 5.4 Regression of Utility Performance on State, Utility, and Corporate Governance Variables, 2010

		Dependent variable: Profit per unit excluding subsidies (2010)—All utilities				
State-level controls	GDP per capita, 2009	0.454	0.463	0.416	0.421	0.442
		(0.167)***	(0.154)***	(0.147)***	(0.151)***	(0.146)***
	Regulatory governance ID index	0.898	0.751	1.031	0.865	0.948
		(0.255)***	(0.243)***	(0.284)***	(0.275)***	(0.277)***
	Regulatory governance IM index	0.358	0.391	−0.267	0.372	−0.233
		(0.731)	(0.753)	(0.701)	(0.675)	(0.777)
Utility-level controls	Discom dummy	−0.666	−0.695	−0.57	−0.619	−0.634
		(0.195)***	(0.180)***	(0.186)***	(0.191)***	(0.181)***
	Net fixed assets, 2009	−0.199	−0.072	−0.078	−0.094	−0.064
		(0.084)***	(0.065)	(0.076)	(0.08)	(0.068)
	Profit per unit, 2007	0.393	0.303	0.31	0.365	0.265
		(0.179)**	(0.169)*	(0.168)*	(0.172)**	(0.16)
Corporate governance variables	Basic CG index	0.274				
		(0.467)				
	Share of board that is executive directors		−0.83			−0.688
			(0.347)**			(0.346)*
	Share of board that is independent directors			1.279		1.088
				(0.566)**		(0.550)*
	Number of directors on board				0.026	
					(0.027)	
	Constant	−3.994	−4.794	−4.422	−4.731	−4.509
		(1.444)***	(1.491)***	(1.488)***	(1.463)***	(1.480)***
	R^2	0.48	0.48	0.49	0.47	0.51
	N	61	62	62	63	62

Source: World Bank analysis.
Note: CG = corporate governance; Discom = distribution company; GDP = gross domestic product; ID = institutional design; IM = implementation of mandates; N = number of observations; R^2 = coefficient of determination. Values in parentheses are White standard errors.
Significance level: * = 10 percent, ** = 5 percent, *** = 1 percent.

regulator has been (and, potentially, is likely to be going forward). Some areas of regulatory action would likely improve the utility's operational viability (such as regular tariff revisions to cover costs), while others may have a negative impact on profits (such as clean energy mandates or OA that would draw away large industrial or commercial consumers) so the net effect is not necessarily positive (or, indeed, predictable). Thus the lack of significance of the IM index is not entirely unexpected.

The indicators of CG enter the regression as anticipated. For the regression of utility profits per unit in 2010, both the share of the board that is independent directors and the share of the board that is executive directors are significant, separately and together, with signs consistent with intuition and with the broad findings of the literature and relevant Indian recommendations. Board size and the basic CG index are not significantly different from zero. While the result on executive directors is robust in that the coefficient remains negative, though at a lower level of significance than earlier,

Table 5.5 Regression of Utility Performance on State, Utility, and Corporate Governance Variables, 2011

		Dependent variable: Profit per unit excluding subsidies (2011)—All utilities				
State-level controls	GDP per capita, 2010	0.288	0.318	0.289	0.278	0.313
		(0.143)**	(0.137)**	(0.140)**	(0.138)**	(0.136)**
	Regulatory governance ID index	0.638	0.621	0.77	0.701	0.697
		(0.232)***	(0.222)***	(0.256)***	(0.216)***	(0.263)**
	Regulatory governance IM index	1.197	0.93	0.745	0.972	0.743
		(0.885)	(0.82)	(0.898)	(0.829)	(0.864)
Utility-level controls	Discom dummy	−0.68	−0.704	−0.654	−0.664	−0.689
		(0.126)***	(0.123)***	(0.123)***	(0.125)***	(0.122)***
	Net fixed assets, 2010	−0.095	−0.081	−0.094	−0.103	−0.081
		(0.058)	(0.054)	(0.055)*	(0.058)*	(0.054)
	Profit per unit, 2007	0.254	0.206	0.228	0.251	0.196
		(0.122)**	(0.118)*	(0.116)*	(0.116)**	(0.114)*
Corporate governance variables	Basic CG index	−0.183				
		(0.372)				
	Share of board that is executive directors		−0.522			−0.461
			(0.264)*			(0.289)
	Share of board that is independent directors			0.507		0.327
				(0.39)		(0.428)
	Number of directors on board				0.02	
					(0.024)	
	Constant	−3.376	−3.536	−3.315	−3.337	−3.457
		(1.694)*	(1.549)**	(1.661)*	(1.601)**	(1.555)**
	R^2	0.52	0.54	0.53	0.53	0.55
	N	65	65	65	66	65

Source: World Bank analysis.
Note: CG = corporate governance; Discom = distribution company; GDP = gross domestic product; ID = institutional design; IM = implementation of mandates; N = number of observations; R^2 = coefficient of determination. Values in parentheses are White standard errors.
Significance level: * = 10 percent, ** = 5 percent, *** = 1 percent.

the coefficient on the share of the board that is independent directors completely loses significance when the regression is repeated for 2011 with updated utility controls but the same corporate and regulatory governance variables (as these are features that tend to change minimally over time). Because utility profits are highly correlated over time, this result will need investigation over a longer timeframe than permitted by the data we have. In any event, the relatively small size of the sample means these results should be taken as indicative rather than definitive.

Tables 5.6 and 5.7 present the results of an ordinary least squares regression of utility profits per unit on the set of independent variables used above, excluding the measures of CG. This permits an increase in sample size to 80. The signs on variable coefficients are generally unchanged, although significance varies. The ID index is positive and significant as in the regressions including CG variables, but the IM index of regulatory governance is now significant, separately and, in the regression for 2011, when included with the ID index.

Table 5.6 Regression of Utility Performance on State, Utility, and Regulatory Governance Variables, 2010

Dependent variable: Profit per unit excluding subsidies (2010)—All utilities			
GDP per capita, 2009	0.483	0.48	0.535
	(0.144)***	(0.141)***	(0.150)***
Discom dummy	−0.564	−0.563	−0.568
	(0.169)***	(0.168)***	(0.169)***
Net fixed assets, 2009	−0.107	−0.104	−0.126
	(0.069)	(0.068)	(0.066)*
Profit per unit, 2007	0.371	0.388	0.377
	(0.142)**	(0.147)**	(0.146)**
Regulatory governance ID index	0.714	0.853	
	(0.243)***	(0.268)***	
Regulatory governance IM index	0.724		1.53
	(0.707)		(0.752)**
Constant	−5.218	−4.73	−5.796
	(1.328)***	(1.340)***	(1.429)***
R^2	0.52	0.51	0.49
N	80	80	80

Source: World Bank analysis.
Note: Discom = distribution company; GDP = gross domestic product; ID = institutional design; IM = implementation of mandates; N = number of observations; R^2 = coefficient of determination. Values in parentheses are White standard errors.
Significance level: * = 10 percent, ** = 5 percent, *** = 1 percent.

Table 5.7 Regression of Utility Performance on State, Utility, and Regulatory Governance Variables, 2011

Dependent variable: Profit per unit excluding subsidies (2011)—All utilities			
GDP per capita, 2010	0.265	0.251	0.329
	(0.144)*	(0.140)*	(0.145)**
Discom dummy	−0.582	−0.575	−0.591
	(0.128)***	(0.129)***	(0.128)***
Net fixed assets, 2010	−0.089	−0.074	−0.108
	(0.051)*	(0.052)	(0.050)**
Profit per unit, 2007	0.388	0.425	0.387
	(0.138)***	(0.148)***	(0.141)***
Regulatory governance ID index	0.668	0.95	
	(0.223)***	(0.250)***	
Regulatory governance IM index	1.495		2.262
	(0.843)*		(0.824)***
Constant	−3.595	−2.57	−4.301
	(1.457)**	(1.323)*	(1.489)***
R^2	0.59	0.57	0.57
N	80	80	80

Source: World Bank analysis.
Note: Discom = distribution company; GDP = gross domestic product; ID = institutional design; IM = implementation of mandates; N = number of observations; R^2 = coefficient of determination. Values in parentheses are White standard errors.
Significance level: * = 10 percent, ** = 5 percent, *** = 1 percent.

Notes

1. Profit is measured as the difference between average revenue and average cost.
2. In this analysis, "power" is defined differently for different types of utilities. For discoms, it is the amount of power input into the distribution system; for gencos, the amount of power generated; and, for transcos, the amount of power wheeled by the transmission system. We use power input (that is, purchased) for discoms since that determines the cost they incur.
3. This is because revenues include subsidies booked by the utility in anticipation of being paid by the government for supplying power to specified groups at a price below the cost of supply. With some notable exceptions, subsidies received are almost the same as subsidies booked. Subsidies are generally only received by companies supplying power directly to consumers.
4. As noted, utility and state-level (including regulatory governance) data were collected under the India Power Sector Review.
5. Government "nominee" directors receive relatively less attention in recommendations or the broader CG literature, and it is less clear what relationship we should expect to observe between such directors and performance. Government directors are, broadly, employees of the owner and may thus better represent the owners' interests; however, as literature focusing on state-owned enterprises has noted, government owners often have conflicting interests and may not prioritize efficiency or financial performance. India's CG guidelines (Department of Public Enterprises, Securities and Exchange Board of India Clause 49) limit such directors to two, or one-sixth of board strength, which supports an expectation that a greater share of government directors will be associated with weaker performance.
6. Though the detailed index is available for 21 utilities, one of those utilities is a holding company (GUVNL in Gujarat) and so does not have performance data available. Thus in table 5.2 the only detailed index correlation that includes this data point is the one with gross domestic product per capita.

CHAPTER 6

Conclusions

This review has presented one of the first in-depth empirical analyses of corporate and regulatory governance of Indian power utilities at the state level. Several welcome findings emerge, including the overarching sense that the initiatives taken by the government on both fronts are steps in the right direction. However, while implementation has varied across the country, for the majority of utilities and states and the country as a whole, governance needs to improve, especially if it is to bring about a more accountable, commercially oriented culture in the sector, improve the efficiency of service delivery, and contribute to the sector's overall financial and operational sustainability.

Corporate Governance

Unbundling the state electricity boards has progressed quite well on paper, although actual separation and functional independence of the unbundled entities are considerably less than appears. While unbundling per se would not necessarily be expected to result in a commercial orientation, the objective of being able to clearly identify the contributions of individual entities in the service value chain and hold them accountable for their performance remains unmet to the extent unbundling is incomplete.

Boards remain state dominated, lack sufficient decision-making authority in practice, and are rarely evaluated on performance. Utilities tend to have more government and executive directors than recommended and fewer independent directors. In fact, only 16 percent of utilities have the recommended share of independent directors, and several lack independent directors entirely. The data analysis, while preliminary, strongly supports the idea that fewer executive directors (that is, separation of management from the board) is desirable because it tends to improve performance—consistent with both international and Indian corporate governance (CG) guidelines. A slightly weaker but still positive result is that an increase in the share of independent directors on corporate utility boards is associated with better performance. Thus many utilities may benefit from adding more independent directors.

Political interference in board appointments and decision making on business aspects remains common. The chairman and managing director (CMD) and board's autonomy is constrained by the state government's involvement in key recruitment, personnel, procurement, and enforcement decisions, underlining the fact that the desired arm's-length relationship between the utility and government has not been achieved. In addition, CMD tenures are often so limited that many CMDs are unlikely to be able to see through implementation of their agendas. Finally, board member training and peer evaluation are conspicuous by their absence. Professionalizing and empowering boards should hence be a key priority going forward.

The analysis shows that going beyond the Companies Act requirements and implementing the practices recommended by the Department of Public Enterprises (DPE) (and even going beyond those to effect organizational transformation) is associated with significantly higher profits per unit, indicating a potential win-win. Few utilities have put the necessary processes in place to support their governance structures. For example, only about one-third have an advanced management information system, and no utility has a corporate performance monitoring system. The limited set of utilities that have developed information-driven processes and sound mechanisms for performance management and that make their accounts and audits publicly available tend to be the top financial performers with high operational efficiency.

As pointed out by an experienced observer and former regulator, the internal governance agenda has to be a priority going forward: "The sector today faces significant challenges. Backlog of investments and inadequate increase in tariffs are often cited as the key reasons for such trends. However, acute deficiency in managerial and organizational capacity is an equally important and often ignored cause of the present problems. Reforms at the state levels should have been accompanied by an organizational transformation of unbundled entities that aims to equip them with adequate systems and processes to cope with the changes witnessed by the sector" (Bajaj 2012).

Regulatory Governance

State electricity regulatory commissions (SERCs) have been established in all states, though some as late as 2011. They are expected to prevent political interference in the sector and protect the interests of different stakeholders by regulating the operations of power utilities and the tariff chargeable to consumers, but they face an enormous challenge in that almost all of the utilities they regulate remain state owned. This can limit the effectiveness of standard regulatory mechanisms, which need to be adapted to the incentive structure of public enterprises.

The ability of SERCs to carry out their mandates depends on the technical, financial, and human resources available to them, their competence, their autonomy in decision making (including, most importantly, insulation from

Conclusions

political pressures), and their accountability. The analysis carried out in this review shows that there is a significant positive association between these features of institutional design and utility profits per unit, which underlines how important a robust regulatory framework is for utility operations.

However, this review also finds that most SERCs are still some way from an institutional design that would permit them to effectively implement their mandates. Most importantly, there is no clear accountability mechanism to govern SERCs themselves—the state legislatures, to whom SERCs nominally report, do not play an active monitoring role, and the Appellate Tribunal, which arguably brings SERCs under the purview of the judicial system, does not have a mandate to routinely monitor regulatory activity or hold SERCs accountable. In addition, SERCs have generally struggled to achieve true autonomy from state governments, in part because of relationships built into the Electricity Act of 2003 (EA 2003) itself. Many SERCs also lack the resources that might assist in performing their functions—most notably, enough professional staff and appropriate information technology systems. Finally, most SERCs have yet to implement adequate transparency measures and create frameworks for meaningful public input to the regulatory process, although a few have institutionalized mechanisms for participatory decision making that are best practice. All these aspects of institutional design have knock-on effects in terms of SERCs' perceived legitimacy, their willingness to take initiative, and the soft power they are able to wield.

The study has also reviewed SERC performance on implementation of their mandates as of 2010, covering six key areas identified in the governing legislation: tariffs, standards of performance (SoP), protection of consumer rights, open access (OA), renewable energy, and regulation in other areas. It found that aside from a few standouts, most SERCs have not yet fully implemented the mandates given them in the EA 2003.

Tariffs cover average cost in a majority of states, but increases in tariffs have generally not kept pace with cost increases and very few states issue multiyear tariffs. Only five SERCs have ever conducted a cost of supply study. SoP have been notified by almost all SERCs—but only 75 percent monitor compliance, and only two have ever imposed a penalty for default. Most SERCs are complying with mandates to promote consumer empowerment and increase transparency to the public but need to do far more to ensure that consumers are given opportunities to engage and that high-quality information is available to the public. Going beyond the EA 2003, 10 SERCs have reported establishing consumer advocacy cells—a bright spot on the landscape.

Finally, though most SERCs have notified most of the key regulations necessary to enact the mandates of the EA 2003, many SERCs have yet to take concrete steps to actually implement these regulations. For example, only half of states have even received an OA application, and only 10 states have actually implemented OA for an applicant. On renewable energy and energy efficiency, most states have notified basic renewable purchase obligation regulations, but only 18 monitor compliance, and only 4 have issued penalties for noncompliance. Significantly fewer states have passed demand-side management, feed-in-tariff, or time-of-day regulations.

Recommendations

The agendas on corporate governance and regulatory governance are urgent and need substantial further action. Establishing an arm's-length relationship between the state and the regulator and the state and the utility, as intended by the reforms initiated decades ago, is still a priority for the sector. Examples of state-owned utilities in West Bengal and Gujarat show that this is possible even with state ownership.

Complete financial and operational unbundling is a critical step in improving the accountability of each unit in the sector value chain.[1] This can help identify where inefficiencies or performance shortfalls occur and, by thus increasing accountability, improve incentives for performance. Full vertical unbundling with separation of accounts, staff, and decision making is also a necessary step toward competition in supply. Since unbundling on its own will not lead to commercialization, it is also important to consider other ways of bringing in efficiencies—for example, divesting an ownership share to central public sector undertakings such as the National Thermal Power Corporation or the Power Grid Corporation of India, which are recognized for strong results and which, as equity owners, might have both an interest in pushing for better performance and the ability to do so. Another option is to start with hardwired limits (through articles of association or other mechanisms) that specify CMD terms and areas in which the board is solely responsible for decisions and restrict interference in both. Of course, the efficacy of any such mechanism depends on the extent to which it can be enforced.

The stock market can be an effective monitoring and enforcement mechanism for governance of listed companies—and has been used with some success in the case of minority-listed central state-owned enterprises. By making the utility transparently answerable to entities other than the state government, stock market listing can limit the state government's ability to interfere with utilities' commercial operations. A first step toward minority listing is to mandate that utilities comply with requirements for listing ("shadow" listing) as a precondition for central or other support.[2] This would imply compliance with the DPE or Securities and Exchange Board of India CG guidelines, which would bring greater autonomy and accountability to boards of state utilities.[3] This would also pave the way for listing if utility performance improves to the requisite level down the road. West Bengal has used "shadow" listing (see box 3.4); the improvement in operational and financial performance of its utilities has been ascribed to the ensuing arm's-length distance between the utility and the state government.

Even in the absence of listing, it will be important to insulate utility operations from state interference: professionalizing and empowering utility boards, reducing the number of executive directors, and bringing in more independent directors, as prescribed in guidelines for CG of central public sector undertakings issued by the DPE, would be a good start. Further, independent directors should be appointed by a committee that includes entities such as the Central Electricity Authority or other representatives of the public interest to avoid capture by the state government.

The use of a memorandum of understanding (MoU) between the utility and the state government that establishes performance targets for the utility along with indicators of achievement can provide a mechanism for the state government to monitor progress toward those targets. The central government currently has MoUs with central public sector enterprises, and though there is considerable room for improvement, MoUs can be a useful tool for motivating performance (World Bank 2006). Beyond India, MoUs or other performance contracts have been used to improve accountability and performance of state-owned enterprises. For MoUs to work, though, appropriate performance targets with well defined, measurable indicators, a transparent means of monitoring progress, and clear and credible consequences for nonachievement are all necessary. Box 6.1 reviews international experience with performance contracts, the characteristics of MoUs in India and key areas for improvement in their implementation.

Regulatory initiative will only arise when regulators are held accountable for their actions. It appears that SERCs do not always take actions necessary to promote long-term sector viability unless they are compelled to. For example, most SERCs have the leeway to determine the tariff on a *suo moto* basis even if the utility does not file an annual revenue requirement; however, few SERCs have actually taken up cases in this manner, partly due to a lack of legislative clarity on when SERCs should initiate *suo moto* action but largely due to a lack of initiative among SERCs. Thus autonomy, while important, is unlikely to be sufficient on its own for achieving results.

One idea is to extend the mandate of the Appellate Tribunal to include a provision for regular monitoring of regulators; another is to use the Planning Commission for periodic evaluation of state regulators, as proposed in the Shunglu Committee report. Regular monitoring by peers in the Forum of Regulators, with full public disclosure of findings, is also worth exploring. In this vein, there is a need for greater public involvement and debate on regulatory issues. Social accountability institutions can play an important role in scrutinizing regulatory performance, especially if quality data on SoP, quality, reliability of service, and so on is regularly collected, analyzed, and made easily accessible. For instance, the Electricity Governance Initiative has developed a toolkit to assess policy and regulatory processes, benchmark best practice, and promote accountability among electricity governance institutions that could be used to develop a comprehensive monitoring framework for regulators (Dixit and others 2007).

In the end, the real challenge is to improve service delivery, for which the link between good service and utility earnings needs to be strengthened. This is likely to require action beyond the governance environment of the utilities, as has been noted: "In hindsight, the weakness of the Indian power reform program has

Box 6.1 MoUs

Memorandums of understanding (MoUs) or other performance contracts between state-owned enterprises (SOEs) and governments have been used to enhance firm performance in several countries, including India, where MoUs are negotiated between all central public sector enterprises (CPSEs) and the government as owner. These set performance targets for SOE boards (forming the basis for a performance management framework and monitoring system) and define the roles, responsibilities, and accountability of the board and entity management. Similar practices are followed in South Africa, Bulgaria, Indonesia, Turkey, and Bangladesh (World Bank 2006).

Historically, performance agreements have had limited success. One common issue has been inappropriate objectives. Certain targets, such as revenue growth and some other financial targets, can create perverse incentives if not thought through. In addition, firm managers typically have greater knowledge of the firm than their government counterparts, which enables them to negotiate easy—and therefore less meaningful—targets. Another issue limiting the success of performance contracts is the introduction of the contracts in isolation, without the accompaniment of wider SOE governance reforms (World Bank 2006). Research has posited that effectively designing and enforcing a performance contract can be as politically costly as well-executed privatization and that performance contracts are therefore not likely to be successful in countries that lack the political will to privatize (Shirley 1998).

Internationally, successful performance contracts appear to be ones that feature sensible targets and sufficiently strong incentives to achieve the targets, set longer terms, and are negotiated with SOEs in relatively more competitive industries (Shirley and Xu 2001).

Compared with most other countries, India has a relatively sophisticated performance contract system that has become a key tool for ensuring accountability of CPSEs and their directors. MoUs are negotiated and signed annually between all CPSEs and the relevant administrative ministry (World Bank 2006). MoU contents follow the Department of Public Enterprises (DPE) guidelines and include a mission statement, the objectives of the CPSE, areas where power has been designated to the CPSE, performance targets, and commitments from the government to the CPSE. In practice, the performance targets are the primary focus of system participants, and DPE guidelines go so far as to specify particular financial and nonfinancial or dynamic targets.

There is, however, room for improvement (World Bank 2010). Targets could be more ambitious, and the DPE task forces that facilitate negotiation of the MoUs could have stronger financial and management skills. In addition, social objectives and service delivery targets could be factored in more prominently, and compliance with corporate governance guidelines could also be included as a criterion for evaluating performance.

---

been that while it has focused appropriately on sorting out distortions in the relationship between the owner-government and power utilities through the unbundling and regulation model, it has failed to carry credible assurances that this will improve the equation between the reformed utilities and their consumers" (Lal 2006, 24).

Notes

1. Separate distribution from transmission if the utility (state utility board) is large enough to warrant this and if managerial capacity is not a constraint (EA 2003 mandates separation of generation from transmission).
2. It is unlikely that there would be much appetite or take-up in a flotation of shares for minority listing of most state-level utilities now.
3. While the existence of CG guidelines differentiates India from many other developing countries, there is still room to strengthen them. For example, the guidelines could specify the principles governing the relationship between the government ministries and the covered companies, and include a system to monitor compliance with the guidelines and clarify which are mandatory and which are voluntary. See World Bank (2010) for more elaboration.

References

Bajaj, Jagmohan L. 2012. "Suggestions for Reforming the Indian Power Sector." Unpublished manuscript.

Dixit, Shantanu, Navroz K. Dubash, Crescencia Maurer, and Smita Nakhooda. 2007. "Benchmarking Best Practice and Promoting Accountability in the Electricity Sector." The Electricity Governance Initiative, World Resources Institute, Washington, DC.

Lal, Sumir. 2006. "Can Good Economics Ever Be Good Politics? Case Study of India's Power Sector." Working Paper 83, World Bank, Washington, DC.

Shirley, Mary. 1998. "Why Performance Contracts for State-Owned Enterprises Haven't Worked." Viewpoint Note 150, World Bank, Washington, DC.

Shirley, Mary, and Lixin Colin Xu. 2001. "Empirical Effects of Performance Contracts: Evidence from China." *Journal of Law, Economics, and Organization* 17 (1).

World Bank. 2006. *Held by the Invisible Hand: The Challenge of State-Owned Enterprise Corporate Governance for Emerging Markets.* Washington, DC: World Bank.

———. 2010. *Corporate Governance of Central Public Sector Enterprises.* Washington, DC: World Bank.

APPENDIX A

Corporate Governance Requirements in India

The guidelines set out by the Securities and Exchange Board of India (SEBI) and the Department of Public Enterprises (DPE) go well beyond the requirements of the Companies Act (which are mandatory) and are generally considered recommended practice for Indian state level public enterprises. The guidelines cover board composition, policies, and training; general board functioning; detailed requirements for audit committees; the government-board relationship; and disclosure. Their provisions are as follows:

Board Composition. Executive or "full-time" directors[1] should comprise no more than 50 percent of the board. There should be no more than two government representatives, and such directors should be less than one-sixth of the board. If the chair is a nonexecutive (executive) director, at least one-third (50 percent) of the board should be independent directors.

Directors cannot be members of more than 10 committees on a single board and cannot hold more than five committee chairs across all of their directorships. Chairpersons should retire by age 62. Independent directors' tenure should be limited to a total of nine years. They should have graduate degrees, at least 10 years of relevant, high-level experience, and should ideally be between 45 and 65 years old (though as old as 72 may be acceptable).

Board Functioning. Boards should meet at least four times per year, with no more than three to four months between any two meetings. They should have a code of conduct that is published online. They should conduct peer evaluations of nonexecutive board members. The company should have procedures to inform board members about risk assessment and minimization policies. They should train board members in the company's business model, the risk profile of its business parameters, and the directors' responsibilities and the best way to discharge them. Boards should have a formal charter that clarifies the roles and responsibilities between individual directors and between the board and management.

Audit Committee. Every board should have an audit committee with at least three members, two-thirds of which, including the chairperson, must be independent directors. All members should be able to read and understand basic financial statements and at least one member should have accounting or related financial management expertise. The audit committee should meet at least four times a year, with no more than four months between any two meetings. Both SEBI and the DPE also define appropriate powers and roles for the audit committee.

Government-Board Relationship and Disclosure. Companies should include a corporate governance (CG) section in their annual reports, which should cover compliance with CG recommended and mandatory practices. SEBI also provides a lengthy set of items recommended for inclusion in this section. There should be clarity about where the board has decision-making powers and where the board must seek government approval.

Although the DPE guidelines are optional for state electricity utilities, they are mandatory for Indian central public sector undertakings (CPSUs), which include centrally owned public sector electricity utilities. Central and state utilities are differentiated not only by such ownership but also by such legal requirements—most notably, CPSUs have to comply with the DPE's CG guidelines—and their market participation (many of the CPSUs are minority-listed on the stock exchange). They also have memorandums of understanding (MoUs) with their government owners, which set performance targets for the utility boards (forming the basis for a performance management framework and monitoring system) and define the roles, responsibilities, and accountability of the board and the utility management. Perhaps as a result, CPSUs tend to exhibit stronger financial performance.

CG has been a key aspect of the Government of India's efforts at CPSU reform, aimed at improving the companies' performance and competitiveness, giving them easier access to capital markets, and making them more transparent and accountable, while also transitioning the state's role from day-to-day manager to a more traditional owner operating through strong CG principles (World Bank 2010). Consistent with the DPE's CG guidelines, the CPSUs follow many of the same CG practices as India's private sector firms, including having independent board members—some with private sector experience—and providing extensive information to the public. The CPSUs' MoUs with the government serve to both monitor and motivate performance.

Potentially as a result of these reforms, performance of CPSUs has strengthened in recent years; for example, NTPC Ltd. (a power generation company), India's largest CPSU, was the second-most profitable central public sector enterprise in 2009, generating about Rs 83,096 million in profits. In 2010, it became one of only four companies to be awarded "Maharatna" status, a title that gives public-sector companies greater autonomy over their investments and participation in global capital markets. NTPC is notable for its high efficiency levels (particularly relative to other generation companies in India), which lead it to generate 27 percent of India's power despite representing only 18 percent of the total national generation capacity.[2]

Broad reviews of India's centrally owned enterprises suggest, however, that there is still room for CG improvements (World Bank 2010). As with the state level utilities, a complex ownership relationship means that the ownership and policy-making roles are combined in some Ministries, which enables political interference in board composition and operational decision making. In addition, CPSE boards are rarely evaluated on their performance (perhaps suggesting a need to strengthen their MoUs) and, in several cases, it has been recommended that they strengthen their internal audit and control functions.

Notes

1. Sometimes known as "functional" directors, they are typically drawn from senior management of the company (such as directors of finance, human resources, and so on).
2. See http://www.ntpc.co.in/index.php?option=com_content&view=article&id=42&Itemid=75&lang=en, accessed May 5, 2013.

Reference

World Bank. 2010. *Corporate Governance of Central Public Sector Enterprises*. Washington, DC: World Bank.

APPENDIX B

Coverage of Electricity Utilities

Table B.1 shows all of the utilities covered in the corporate governance review, including their full name, the abbreviation employed in this review, their "type" (discom, transco, genco, or holding company), and if they are covered in the basic dataset and in the detailed dataset.

Table B.1 Coverage of Electricity Utilities

State	Utility name	Abbreviation	Type	Basic data	Detailed data
Andhra Pradesh	Andhra Pradesh Central Power Distribution Company Ltd.	APCPDCL	Discom	Y	Y
Andhra Pradesh	Andhra Pradesh Eastern Power Distribution Company Ltd.	APEPDCL	Discom	Y	N
Andhra Pradesh	Andhra Pradesh Northern Power Distribution Company Ltd.	APNPDCL	Discom	Y	N
Andhra Pradesh	Andhra Pradesh Southern Power Distribution Company Ltd.	APSPDCL	Discom	Y	N
Assam	Assam Electricity Grid Corporation Ltd.	AEGCL	Transco	Y	Y
Assam	Assam Power Distribution Corporation Ltd.	APDCL	Discom	Y	Y
Assam	Assam Power Generation Company Ltd.	APGCL—Assam	Genco	Y	N
Chhattisgarh	Chhattisgarh State Power Distribution Company Ltd.	CSPDCL	Discom	Y	N
Chhattisgarh	Chhattisgarh State Power Generation Company Ltd.	CSPGCL	Genco	Y	N
Chhattisgarh	Chhattisgarh State Power Transmission Company Ltd.	CSPTCL	Transco	Y	N
Delhi	BSES Rajdhani Power Ltd.	BRPL	Discom	Y	N
Delhi	BSES Yamuna Power Ltd.	BYPL	Discom	Y	N
Delhi	Delhi Transco Ltd.	DTL	Transco	Y	Y
Delhi	Indraprastha Power Generation Company Ltd.	IPGCL	Genco	Y	N
Delhi	Pragati Power Corporation Ltd.	PPCL	Genco	Y	N
Delhi	North Delhi Power Ltd.	TP-DDL	Discom	Y	Y
Gujarat	Dakshin Gujarat Vij Company Ltd.	DGVCL	Discom	Y	Y
Gujarat	Gujarat Energy Transmission Corporation Ltd.	GETCL	Transco	Y	N
Gujarat	Gujarat State Electricity Corporation Ltd.	GSECL	Genco	Y	N
Gujarat	Gujarat Urja Vikas Nigam Ltd.	GUVNL	Holding company	Y	Y
Gujarat	Madhya Gujarat Vij Company Ltd.	MGVCL	Discom	Y	N
Gujarat	Paschim Gujarat Vij Company Ltd.	PGVCL	Discom	Y	N
Gujarat	Uttar Gujarat Vij Company Ltd.	UGVCL	Discom	Y	N
Haryana	Dakshin Haryana Bijli Vitran Nigam Ltd	DHBVNL	Discom	Y	N
Haryana	Haryana Power Generation Corporation Ltd.	HPGCL	Genco	Y	N
Haryana	Haryana Vidyut Prasaran Nigam Ltd.	HVPNL	Transco	Y	N
Haryana	Uttar Haryana Bijli Vitran Nigam Ltd.	UHBVN	Discom	Y	Y
Himachal Pradesh	Himachal Pradesh State Electricity Board Ltd.	HPSEB LTD	Discom	Y	N
Other	Other State Power Development Corporation Ltd.	Other SPDCL	Genco	Y	N

table continues next page

Table B.1 Coverage of Electricity Utilities *(continued)*

State	Utility name	Abbreviation	Type	Basic data	Detailed data
Karnataka	Chamundeshwari Electricity Supply Company Ltd.	CESCOM	Discom	Y	N
Karnataka	Gulbarga Electricity Supply Company Ltd.	GESCOM	Discom	Y	N
Karnataka	Hubli Electricity Supply Company Ltd.	HESCOM	Discom	Y	N
Karnataka	Karnataka Power Transmission Company Ltd.	KPTCL	Transco	Y	Y
Karnataka	Mangalore electricity Supply Company Ltd.	MESCOM	Discom	Y	N
Madhya Pradesh	Madhya Pradesh Madhya Kshetra Vidyut Vitaran Company Ltd.	MPMKVVCL	Discom	Y	Y
Madhya Pradesh	Madhya Pradesh Paschim Kshetra Vidyut Vitaran Company Ltd.	MPPaKVVCL	Discom	Y	N
Madhya Pradesh	Madhya Pradesh Power Generation Company Ltd.	MPPGCL	Genco	Y	N
Madhya Pradesh	Madhya Pradesh Poorva Kshetra Vidyut Vitaran Company Ltd.	MPPoKVVCL	Discom	Y	N
Madhya Pradesh	Madhya Pradesh Power Transmission Company Ltd.	MPPTCL	Transco	Y	Y
Maharashtra	Maharashtra State Electricity Distribution Company Ltd.	MSEDCL	Discom	Y	Y
Maharashtra	Maharashtra State Electricity Transmission Company Ltd.	MSETCL	Transco	Y	N
Maharashtra	Maharashtra State Power Generation Company Ltd.	MSPGCL	Genco	Y	Y
Orissa	Grid Corporation of Orissa Ltd.	GRIDCO	Transco	Y	N
Orissa	North Eastern Electricity Supply Company	NESCO	Discom	Y	N
Orissa	Orissa Hydro Power Corporation	OHPC	Genco	Y	N
Orissa	Orissa Power Generation Corporation	OPGC	Genco	Y	N
Orissa	Orissa Power Transmission Corporation Ltd.	OPTCL	Transco	Y	N
Orissa	Southern Electricity Supply Company	SOUTHCO	Discom	Y	N
Orissa	Western Electricity Supply Company	WESCO	Discom	Y	N
Punjab	Punjab State Power Corporation Ltd.	PSPCL	Discom	Y	Y
Punjab	Punjab State Transmission Corporation Ltd.	PSTCL	Transco	Y	N
Rajasthan	Ajmer Vidyut Vitran Nigam Ltd.	AVVNL	Discom	Y	N
Rajasthan	Jodhpur Vidyut Vitran Nigam Ltd.	JoVVNL	Discom	Y	N
Rajasthan	Jaipur Vidyut Vitran Nigam Ltd.	JVVNL	Discom	Y	Y
Rajasthan	Rajasthan Rajya Vidyut Utpadan Nigam Ltd.	RRVUNL	Genco	Y	N
Rajasthan	Rajasthan Rajya Vidyut Prasaran Nigam Ltd.	RVPNL	Transco	Y	Y
Tamil Nadu	Tamil Nadu Generation and Distribution Corporation Ltd.	TANGEDCO	Discom	Y	Y
Tripura	Tripura State Electricity Corporation Ltd.	TSECL	Discom[a]	Y	N

table continues next page

Table B.1 Coverage of Electricity Utilities *(continued)*

State	Utility name	Abbreviation	Type	Basic data	Detailed data
Uttar Pradesh	Kanpur Electric Supply Company	KESCO	Discom	Y	N
Uttar Pradesh	Madhyanchal Vidyut Vitran Nigam Ltd.	MVVNL	Discom	Y	Y
Uttar Pradesh	Uttar Pradesh Jal Vidyut Nigam Ltd.	UPJVNL	Genco	Y	N
Uttar Pradesh	Uttar Pradesh Power Transmission Corporation Ltd.	UPPTCL	Transco	Y	Y
Uttar Pradesh	Uttar Pradesh Rajya Vidyut Utpadan Nigam Ltd.	UPRVUNL	Genco	Y	N
Uttarakhand	Power Transmission Corporation of Uttarakhand Ltd.	PTCUL	Transco	Y	N
Uttarakhand	Uttarakhand Jal Vidyut Nigam Ltd.	UJVNL	Genco	Y	N
Uttarakhand	Uttarakhand Power Corporation Ltd.	UPCL	Discom	Y	N
West Bengal	West Bengal Power Development Corporation Ltd.	WBPDCL	Genco	Y	N
West Bengal	West Bengal State Electricity Distribution Company Ltd.	WBSEDCL	Discom	Y	Y
West Bengal	West Bengal State Electricity Transmission Company Ltd.	WBSETCL	Transco	Y	Y

Source: World Bank compilation based on Government of India data.
Note: Discom = distribution company; Genco = generation company; Transco = transmission company; N = no; Y = yes.
a. TSECL is actually a corporation that performs all three functions—generation, transmission, and distribution—but, as noted in the main text, it is categorized as a discom for the purposes of this review.

APPENDIX C

Utility Performance on Corporate Governance Indexes

Table C.1 lists each utility's score on the basic and detailed (if applicable) corporate governance indexes.

Table C.1 Basic and Detailed Index Scores

State	Utility	Type	Basic index score (%)	Detailed index score (%)
Andhra Pradesh	APCPDCL	Discom	75	44
Andhra Pradesh	APEPDCL	Discom	75	
Andhra Pradesh	APNPDCL	Discom	75	
Andhra Pradesh	APSPDCL	Discom	88	
Assam	AEGCL	Transco	88	44
Assam	APDCL	Discom	100	44
Assam	APGCL	Genco	88	
Chhattisgarh	CSPDCL	Discom	50	
Chhattisgarh	CSPGCL	Genco	50	
Chhattisgarh	CSPTCL	Transco	50	
Delhi	BRPL	Discom	50	
Delhi	BYPL	Discom	50	
Delhi	DTL	Transco	50	44
Delhi	IPGCL	Genco	75	
Delhi	PPCL	Genco	75	
Delhi	TP-DDL	Discom	50	67
Gujarat	DGVCL	Discom	88	89
Gujarat	GETCL	Transco	75	
Gujarat	GSECL	Genco	75	
Gujarat	GUVNL	Holding company	100	89
Gujarat	MGVCL	Discom	75	
Gujarat	PGVCL	Discom	50	
Gujarat	UGVCL	Discom	75	
Haryana	DHBVNL	Discom	63	

table continues next page

Table C.1 Basic and Detailed Index Scores *(continued)*

State	Utility	Type	Basic index score (%)	Detailed index score (%)
Haryana	HPGCL	Genco	63	
Haryana	HVPNL	Transco	75	
Haryana	UHBVN	Discom	50	28
Himachal Pradesh	HPSEB LTD	Discom	75	
Other	Other SPDCL	Genco	50	
Karnataka	CESCOM	Discom	75	
Karnataka	GESCOM	Discom	50	
Karnataka	HESCOM	Discom	63	
Karnataka	KPTCL	Transco	63	56
Karnataka	MESCOM	Discom	38	
Madhya Pradesh	MPMKVVCL	Discom	63	56
Madhya Pradesh	MPPaKVVCL	Discom	88	
Madhya Pradesh	MPPGCL	Genco	50	
Madhya Pradesh	MPPoKVVCL	Discom	88	
Madhya Pradesh	MPPTCL	Transco	63	44
Maharashtra	MSEDCL	Discom	75	56
Maharashtra	MSETCL	Transco	50	
Maharashtra	MSPGCL	Genco	75	61
Orissa	GRIDCO	Transco		
Orissa	NESCO	Discom	50	
Orissa	OHPC	Genco	88	
Orissa	OPGC	Genco	75	
Orissa	OPTCL	Transco	50	
Orissa	SOUTHCO	Discom	50	
Orissa	WESCO	Discom	50	
Punjab	PSPCL	Discom	50	33
Punjab	PSTCL	Transco		
Rajasthan	AVVNL	Discom	63	
Rajasthan	JoVVNL	Discom	63	
Rajasthan	JVVNL	Discom	50	33
Rajasthan	RRVUNL	Genco	63	
Rajasthan	RVPNL	Transco	63	33
Tamil Nadu	TANGEDCO	Discom	38	22
Tripura	TSECL	Discom	38	
Uttar Pradesh	KESCO	Discom	50	
Uttar Pradesh	MVVNL	Discom	50	22
Uttar Pradesh	UPJVNL	Genco	38	
Uttar Pradesh	UPPTCL	Transco	50	28
Uttar Pradesh	UPRVUNL	Genco	75	
Uttarakhand	PTCUL	Transco	50	
Uttarakhand	UJVNL	Genco	63	
Uttarakhand	UPCL	Discom	50	
West Bengal	WBPDCL	Genco	88	
West Bengal	WBSEDCL	Discom	88	72
West Bengal	WBSETCL	Transco	88	72

Source: Based on Government of India data.
Note: The detailed index is limited to the 21 utilities for which in-depth corporate governance data was collected. See chapter 3 for more detail. Discom = distribution company; Genco = generation company; Transco = transmission company.

APPENDIX D

Corporate Governance Data

Table D.1 displays all of the data points included in the basic corporate governance index.

Table D.2 displays all of the data points included in the detailed corporate governance index. All of the data points included in the basic index are also included in the detailed index, and therefore some of the data from table D.1 is also included in this table.

Table D.1 Basic Corporate Governance Data

State	Utility	Share of board that is executive directors (%)	Number of government directors	Share of board that is independent directors (%)	Executive chairman[a]	Board size	Audit committee	External auditor	Audit made public	Accounts made public
Andhra Pradesh	APCPDCL	71	2	0	Y	7	Y	Y	Y	Y
Andhra Pradesh	APEPDCL	56	2	22	Y	9	Y	Y	Y	Y
Andhra Pradesh	APNPDCL	56	2	22	Y	9	Y	Y	Y	Y
Andhra Pradesh	APSPDCL	43	2	29	Y	7	Y	Y	Y	Y
Assam	AEGCL	13	3	50	N	8	Y	Y	Y	Y
Assam	APDCL	14	2	57	Y	7	Y	Y	Y	Y
Assam	APGCL	13	4	38	N	8	Y	Y	N	Y
Chhattisgarh	CSPDCL	0	4	0	N	4	N	Y	N	Y
Chhattisgarh	CSPGCL	0	4	0	N	4	N	Y	N	Y
Chhattisgarh	CSPTCL	0	4	0	N	4	N	Y	N	Y
Delhi	BRPL	14	3	29	N	7	Y	Y	N	N
Delhi	BYPL	14	3	29	N	7	Y	Y	N	N
Delhi	DTL	50	3	13	Y	8	Y	Y	N	N
Delhi	IPGCL	43	3	14	N	7	Y	Y	N	Y
Delhi	PPCL	43	3	14	N	7	Y	Y	Y	Y
Delhi	TP-DDL	9	5	18	Y	11	Y	Y	N	N
Gujarat	DGVCL	14	3	43	N	7	Y	Y	Y	Y
Gujarat	GETCL	14	5	14	N	7	Y	Y	Y	Y
Gujarat	GSECL	13	6	13	N	8	Y	Y	Y	Y
Gujarat	GUVNL	33	2	33	N	6	Y	Y	Y	Y
Gujarat	MGVCL	17	5	0	N	6	Y	Y	Y	Y
Gujarat	PGVCL	10	8	10	N	10	Y	Y	N	N
Gujarat	UGVCL	11	7	11	N	9	Y	Y	Y	Y
Haryana	DHBVNL	50	4	0	N	8	Y	Y	N	Y
Haryana	HPGCL	33	4	22	N	9	Y	Y	N	Y
Haryana	HVPNL	33	4	33	N	12	Y	Y	N	Y
Haryana	UHBVN	43	4	0	N	7	Y	Y	N	N

table continues next page

Table D.1 Basic Corporate Governance Data *(continued)*

State	Utility	Share of board that is executive directors (%)	Number of government directors	Share of board that is independent directors (%)	Executive chairman[a]	Board size	Audit committee	External auditor	Audit made public	Accounts made public
Himachal Pradesh	HPSEB LTD	71	2	0	Y	7	Y	Y	Y	Y
Other	Other SPDCL	30	6	10	N	10	Y	Y	N	N
Karnataka	CESCOM	18	9	0	N	11	Y	Y	Y	Y
Karnataka	GESCOM	18	9	0	N	11	Y	Y	N	N
Karnataka	HESCOM	23	10	0	N	13	Y	Y	Y	Y
Karnataka	KPTCL	27	10	7	N	15	Y	Y	Y	Y
Karnataka	MESCOM	60	2	0	Y	5	Y	Y	N	N
Madhya Pradesh	MPMKVVCL	11	5	33	N	9	Y	Y	N	N
Madhya Pradesh	MPPaKVVCL	33	2	33	Y	6	Y	Y	Y	Y
Madhya Pradesh	MPPGCL	33	3	33	Y	9	Y	Y	N	N
Madhya Pradesh	MPPoKVVCL	33	2	33	Y	6	Y	Y	Y	Y
Madhya Pradesh	MPPTCL	17	3	33	N	6	Y	Y	N	N
Maharashtra	MSEDCL	44	3	22	Y	9	Y	Y	Y	Y
Maharashtra	MSETCL	80	1	0	Y	5	Y	Y	N	N
Maharashtra	MSPGCL	83	1	0	N	6	Y	Y	Y	Y
Orissa	NESCO	11	4	0	N	9	Y	Y	N	N
Orissa	OHPC	33	4	33	N	12	Y	Y	Y	Y
Orissa	OPGC	50	3	0	N	6	Y	Y	Y	Y
Orissa	OPTCL	36	3	36	Y	11	Y	Y	Y	N
Orissa	SOUTHCO	11	4	0	N	9	Y	Y	N	N
Orissa	WESCO	11	4	0	N	9	Y	Y	N	N
Punjab	PSPCL	78	2	0	Y	9	Y	Y	N	N
Rajasthan	AVVNL	33	6	0	N	9	Y	Y	N	Y
Rajasthan	JoVVNL	33	6	0	N	9	Y	Y	N	Y
Rajasthan	JVVNL	50	4	0	Y	8	Y	Y	N	N
Rajasthan	RRVUNL	44	5	0	Y	9	Y	Y	N	Y
Rajasthan	RVPNL	57	3	0	Y	7	Y	Y	Y	Y

table continues next page

Table D.1 Basic Corporate Governance Data *(continued)*

State	Utility	Share of board that is executive directors (%)	Number of government directors	Share of board that is independent directors (%)	Executive chairman[a]	Board size	Audit committee	External auditor	Audit made public	Accounts made public
Tamil Nadu	TANGEDCO	56	4	0	Y	9	Y	Y	N	N
Tripura	TSECL	60	2	0	Y	5	N	Y	N	N
Uttar Pradesh	KESCO	20	4	0	N	5	Y	Y	N	N
Uttar Pradesh	MVVNL	75	1	0	N	4	Y	Y	N	N
Uttar Pradesh	UPJVNL	25	6	0	Y	8	N	Y	N	N
Uttar Pradesh	UPPTCL	78	2	0	N	9	Y	Y	N	N
Uttar Pradesh	UPRVUNL	30	6	10	Y	10	Y	Y	Y	Y
Uttarakhand	PTCUL	40	5	10	N	10	Y	Y	N	N
Uttarakhand	UJVNL	27	4	36	N	11	Y	Y	N	N
Uttarakhand	UPCL	42	5	17	N	12	Y	Y	N	N
West Bengal	WBPDCL	44	2	33	Y	9	Y	Y	Y	Y
West Bengal	WBSEDCL	50	2	33	Y	12	Y	Y	Y	Y
West Bengal	WBSETCL	50	2	25	N	8	Y	Y	Y	Y

Source: Based on Government of India data.
a. "Y" indicates if the utility's chair is an executive director, "N" otherwise. This variable was not directly included in the index but was used to determine the threshold for best practice for share of independent directors.

Table D.2 Detailed Corporate Governance Data

		Board-management relationship					Public accountability		Board effectiveness	
State	Utility	Share of board that is executive directors (%)	Audit committee	Other committees	Independent chair of audit committee	Audit on time	Audit made public	Accounts made public	Board size	Average CMD tenure (years)
Andhra Pradesh	APCPDCL	71	Y	N	N	Y	Y	Y	7	1.67
Assam	AEGCL	13	Y	N	N	Y	Y	Y	8	1.69
Assam	APDCL	14	Y	N	N	N	Y	Y	7	1.92
Delhi	DTL	50	Y	N	N	Y	N	N	8	1.05
Delhi	TP-DDL	9	Y	Y	N	Y	N	N	11	5.00
Gujarat	DGVCL	14	Y	Y	Y	Y	Y	Y	7	2.33
Gujarat	GUVNL	33	Y	Y	N	Y	Y	Y	6	2.83
Haryana	UHBVN	43	Y	N	N	Y	N	N	7	1.32
Karnataka	KPTCL	27	Y	Y	N	Y	Y	Y	15	2.33
Madhya Pradesh	MPMKVVCL	11	Y	Y	N	Y	N	N	9	2.00
Madhya Pradesh	MPPTCL	17	Y	N	N	Y	N	N	6	5.00
Maharashtra	MSEDCL	44	Y	Y	N	Y	Y	Y	9	2.00
Maharashtra	MSPGCL	83	Y	Y	N	Y	Y	Y	6	3.50
Punjab	PSPCL	78	Y	Y	N	Y	N	N	9	2.25
Rajasthan	JVVNL	50	Y	Y	N	Y	N	N	8	1.30
Rajasthan	RVPNL	57	Y	N	N	Y	Y	Y	7	1.75
Tamil Nadu	TANGEDCO	56	Y	N	N	Y	N	N	9	2.00
Uttar Pradesh	MVVNL	75	Y	N	N	N	N	N	4	2.00
Uttar Pradesh	UPPTCL	78	Y	Y	N	N	N	N	9	1.30
West Bengal	WBSEDCL	50	Y	Y	Y	Y	Y	Y	12	4.00
West Bengal	WBSETCL	50	Y	Y	Y	Y	Y	Y	8	3.00

Source: Based on Government of India data.

table continues next page

Table D.2 Detailed Corporate Governance Data *(continued)*

		External accountability					Management practices			
State	Utility	Number of government directors	Share of board that is independent directors (%)	External auditor	Government influence (Routine)	Government influence (Recruitments)	ERP or MIS	Performance linked incentives	Employee training policy	Merit-based promotion
Andhra Pradesh	APCPDCL	2	0	Y	Y	Y	Y	N	N	N
Assam	AEGCL	3	50	Y	Y	Y	N	N	N	N
Assam	APDCL	2	57	Y	Y	Y	N	N	N	N
Delhi	DTL	3	13	Y	Y	N	Y	N	Y	N
Delhi	TP-DDL	5	18	Y	N	N	Y	Y	Y	Y
Gujarat	DGVCL	3	43	Y	N	N	Y	Y	Y	Y
Gujarat	GUVNL	2	33	Y	N	N	Y	Y	Y	Y
Haryana	UHBVN	4	0	Y	Y	Y	N	N	N	N
Karnataka	KPTCL	10	7	Y	Y	Y	Y	N	Y	Y
Madhya Pradesh	MPMKVVCL	5	33	Y	Y	N	Y	N	Y	N
Madhya Pradesh	MPPTCL	3	33	Y	Y	N	N	N	Y	N
Maharashtra	MSEDCL	3	22	Y	Y	N	N	N	Y	N
Maharashtra	MSPGCL	1	0	Y	Y	N	Y	N	Y	N
Punjab	PSPCL	2	0	Y	Y	Y	N	N	N	N
Rajasthan	JVVNL	4	0	Y	Y	Y	N	N	N	N
Rajasthan	RVPNL	3	0	Y	Y	Y	N	N	N	N
Tamil Nadu	TANGEDCO	4	0	Y	Y	Y	N	N	Y	N
Uttar Pradesh	MVVNL	1	0	Y	Y	Y	N	N	N	N
Uttar Pradesh	UPPTCL	2	0	Y	Y	Y	N	N	N	N
West Bengal	WBSEDCL	2	33	Y	N	Y	N	N	Y	Y
West Bengal	WBSETCL	2	25	Y	N	Y	N	N	Y	Y

Source: Based on Government of India data.
Note: CMD = chairman and managing director; ERP = enterprise resource planning; MIS = management information system.

APPENDIX E

Coverage of State Electricity Regulatory Commissions

This review covers all of the state electricity regulatory commissions (SERCs) that were established in India as of 2013. Table E.1 lists those SERCs and their abbreviations.

Table E.1 Coverage of SERCs

State	SERC
Andhra Pradesh	APERC
Other	Other SERC
Assam	AERC
Bihar	BERC
Chhattisgarh	CSERC
Delhi	DERC
Goa (joint with Union Territories)	JERC (for Goa and UTs)
Gujarat	GERC
Haryana	HERC
Himachal Pradesh	HPERC
Other	Other SERC
Jharkhand	JSERC
Karnataka	KERC
Kerala	KSERC
Madhya Pradesh	MPERC
Maharashtra	MERC
Manipur and Mizoram	JERC (for Manipur and Mizoram)
Meghalaya	MSERC
Nagaland	NERC
Orissa	OERC
Punjab	PSERC
Rajasthan	RERC
Sikkim	*No name given*
Tamil Nadu	TNERC
Tripura	TERC
Uttar Pradesh	UPERC
Uttarakhand	UERC
West Bengal	WBERC

Source: World Bank compilation.
Note: SERC = state electricity regulatory commission; UT = Union Territory.

APPENDIX F

SERC Performance on Regulatory Governance Indexes

Table F.1 lists state electricity regulatory commission scores on the overall regulatory governance indexes and their subcomponents.

Table F.1 Regulatory Governance Index Scores (%)

	ID	Autonomy	Capacity	Transparency	IM	Tariffs	Consumer protection	SoP	OA	Clean energy	Other regulations
Andhra Pradesh	62	0	100	86	93	75	100	100	100	86	100
Assam	10	0	0	29	76	50	100	75	80	71	80
Bihar	31	50	0	43	71	25	100	75	80	86	60
Chhattisgarh	62	50	50	86	82	75	100	50	100	86	80
Delhi	83	50	100	100	84	75	100	75	80	71	100
Goa	29	0	0	86	54	25	100	75	20	43	60
Gujarat	100	100	100	100	81	50	100	50	100	86	100
Haryana	26	0	50	29	64	25	100	50	80	71	60
Himachal Pradesh	62	100	0	86	88	75	100	75	100	100	80
Other	40	50	0	71	56	25	67	50	60	71	60
Jharkhand	62	100	0	86	81	25	100	100	100	100	60
Karnataka	45	50	0	86	87	75	100	75	100	71	100
Kerala	45	50	0	86	76	75	100	75	80	86	40
Madhya Pradesh	45	50	0	86	86	75	100	75	100	86	80
Maharashtra	83	50	100	100	85	50	100	75	100	86	100
Manipur and Mizoram	29	0	0	86	57	25	100	50	20	86	60
Meghalaya	29	0	0	86	63	25	100	75	60	57	60
Orissa	95	100	100	86	85	75	100	75	100	100	60
Punjab	40	50	0	71	63	25	100	50	100	43	60
Rajasthan	45	50	0	86	76	25	100	75	100	57	100
Tamil Nadu	36	0	50	57	68	0	100	75	80	71	80
Tripura	29	0	0	86	47	50	100	50	20	43	20
Uttar Pradesh	62	50	50	86	70	25	100	75	100	57	60
Uttarakhand	10	0	0	29	75	50	100	75	80	86	60
West Bengal	52	100	0	57	83	75	100	75	100	71	60

Source: World Bank compilation.
Note: ID = institutional design; IM = implementation of mandates; OA = open access; SoP = standards of performance.

APPENDIX G

Regulatory Governance Data

Table G.1 lists the data points included in the regulatory governance institutional design index.

Tables G.2 through G.4 list the data points included in the implementation of regulatory mandates index.

Table G.1 Institutional Design Data

State	Autonomy		Capacity			Transparency					
	SERC budget source	Chair tenure (years)	Number of SERC professional staff	RIMS	Regulations online	Public tariff hearings	Annual reports (Public)	Annual reports (local language)	Annual reports (online)	SAC constitution online	SAC minutes online
Andhra Pradesh	State	4.40	28	Yes	Yes	Yes	Yes	No	Yes	Yes	Yes
Assam	State	1.75	8	No	Yes	Yes	No	No	No	No	No
Bihar	Own Rev.	3.30	8	No	Yes	Yes	No	No	No	Yes	No
Chhattisgarh	Mixed	5.00	22	No	Yes	Yes	Yes	Yes	Yes	Yes	No
Delhi	Mixed	4.30	25	Yes	Yes	Yes	Yes	Yes	Yes	Yes	Yes
Goa	State	4.00	5	No	Yes	Yes	Yes	No	Yes	Yes	Yes
Gujarat	Own Rev.	5.00	25	Yes	Yes	Yes	Yes	Yes	Yes	Yes	Yes
Haryana	State	2.40	15	No	Yes	Yes	No	No	No	No	No
Himachal Pradesh	Mixed	5.00	14	No	Yes	Yes	Yes	Yes	Yes	Yes	No
Other	Mixed	4.00	11	No	Yes	Yes	Yes	No	Yes	Yes	No
Jharkhand	Mixed	5.00	5	No	Yes	Yes	Yes	Yes	Yes	Yes	No
Karnataka	State	5.00	11	No	Yes	Yes	Yes	No	Yes	Yes	Yes
Kerala	Mixed	3.50	4	No	Yes	Yes	Yes	No	Yes	yes	Yes
Madhya Pradesh	Own Rev.	3.75	12	No	Yes	Yes	Yes	Yes	Yes	Yes	No
Maharashtra	Own Rev.	4.30	40	Yes	Yes	Yes	Yes	Yes	Yes	Yes	Yes
Manipur and Mizoram	Mixed	3.00	8	No	Yes	Yes	Yes	No	Yes	Yes	Yes
Meghalaya	State	2.05	6	No	Yes	Yes	Yes	No	Yes	Yes	Yes
Orissa	Mixed	5.00	18	Yes	Yes	Yes	Yes	No	Yes	Yes	Yes
Punjab	State	5.00	8	No	Yes	Yes	Yes	No	Yes	Yes	No
Rajasthan	Own Rev.	4.20	14	No	Yes	Yes	Yes	No	Yes	Yes	Yes
Tamil Nadu	State	4.30	6	Yes	Yes	Yes	No	No	No	Yes	Yes
Tripura	State	4.50	3	No	Yes	Yes	Yes	No	Yes	Yes	Yes
Uttar Pradesh	State	5.00	12	Yes	Yes	Yes	Yes	Yes	Yes	Yes	No
Uttarakhand	State	2.67	11	No	Yes	Yes	No	No	No	No	No
West Bengal	Own Rev.	5.00	8	No	Yes	No	Yes	No	Yes	Yes	No

Source: World Bank compilation.
Note: SERC = state electricity regulatory commission; SAC = state advisory committee; RIMS = Regulatory Information Management System.

Table G.2 Implementation of Mandates Data: Tariffs and Standards of Performance

State	Tariffs				SoP			
	Tariff order delays (number of years with delay)	Percent of years of SERC existence tariff order issued	Tariff at operating-cost-recovery level	MYT order issued	SoP regulations	Penalties for SoP noncompliance	Compliance monitored	SoP penalties issued
Andhra Pradesh	1	100	No	Yes	Yes	Yes	Yes	Yes
Assam	2	60	Yes	Yes	Yes	Yes	Yes	No
Bihar	0	33	No	No	Yes	Yes	Yes	No
Chhattisgarh	0	44	Yes	Yes	Yes	Yes	No	No
Delhi	1	60	Yes	Yes	Yes	Yes	Yes	No
Goa	2	0	Yes	No	Yes	Yes	Yes	No
Gujarat	2	50	Yes	Yes	Yes	Yes	No	No
Haryana	2	100	No	No	Yes	Yes	No	No
Himachal Pradesh	3	70	Yes	Yes	Yes	Yes	Yes	No
Other	1	22	No	No	Yes	Yes	No	No
Jharkhand	0	25	No	No	Yes	Yes	Yes	Yes
Karnataka	2	70	Yes	Yes	Yes	Yes	Yes	No
Kerala	0	78	Yes	No	Yes	Yes	Yes	No
Madhya Pradesh	0	80	Yes	Yes	Yes	Yes	Yes	No
Maharashtra	2	50	Yes	Yes	Yes	Yes	Yes	No
Manipur and Mizoram	1	0	No	No	Yes	Yes	No	No
Meghalaya	2	43	Yes	No	Yes	Yes	Yes	No
Orissa	0	70	Yes	No	Yes	Yes	Yes	No
Punjab	2	80	No	No	Yes	Yes	No	No
Rajasthan	2	20	No	Yes	Yes	Yes	Yes	No
Tamil Nadu	2	10	No	No	Yes	Yes	Yes	No
Tripura	0	29	Yes	No	Yes	Yes	No	No
Uttar Pradesh	2	60	Yes	No	Yes	Yes	Yes	No
Uttarakhand	0	56	Yes	No	Yes	Yes	Yes	No
West Bengal	2	80	Yes	Yes	Yes	Yes	Yes	No

Source: World Bank compilation.
Note: MYT = multiyear tariff; SERC = state electricity regulatory commission; SoP = standards of performance.

Table G.3 Implementation of Mandates Data: Consumer Protection and Other Regulations

State	Consumer protection			Other Regulations				
	Ombudsman	SAC	CGRF regulations	Supply code	Trading	Metering	MYT regulations	ABT
Andhra Pradesh	Yes	Yes	Yes	Yes	Yes	Yes	Yes	Yes
Assam	Yes	Yes	Yes	Yes	Yes	Yes	Yes	No
Bihar	Yes	Yes	Yes	Yes	Yes	Yes	No	No
Chhattisgarh	Yes	Yes	Yes	Yes	Yes	Yes	Yes	No
Delhi	Yes	Yes	Yes	Yes	Yes	Yes	Yes	Yes
Goa	Yes	Yes	Yes	Yes	Yes	Yes	No	No
Gujarat	Yes	Yes	Yes	Yes	Yes	Yes	Yes	Yes
Haryana	Yes	Yes	Yes	Yes	No	Yes	Yes	No
Himachal Pradesh	Yes	Yes	Yes	Yes	Yes	Yes	Yes	No
Other	No	Yes	Yes	Yes	No	Yes	Yes	No
Jharkhand	Yes	Yes	Yes	Yes	Yes	No	Yes	No
Karnataka	Yes	Yes	Yes	Yes	Yes	Yes	Yes	Yes
Kerala	Yes	Yes	Yes	Yes	No	No	Yes	No
Madhya Pradesh	Yes	Yes	Yes	Yes	Yes	Yes	No	Yes
Maharashtra	Yes	Yes	Yes	Yes	Yes	Yes	Yes	Yes
Manipur and Mizoram	Yes	Yes	Yes	Yes	Yes	Yes	No	No
Meghalaya	Yes	Yes	Yes	Yes	Yes	Yes	No	No
Orissa	Yes	Yes	Yes	Yes	No	Yes	No	Yes
Punjab	Yes	Yes	Yes	Yes	Yes	Yes	No	No
Rajasthan	Yes	Yes	Yes	Yes	Yes	Yes	Yes	Yes
Tamil Nadu	Yes	Yes	Yes	Yes	Yes	Yes	Yes	No
Tripura	Yes	Yes	Yes	Yes	No	No	No	No
Uttar Pradesh	Yes	Yes	Yes	Yes	Yes	Yes	No	No
Uttarakhand	Yes	Yes	Yes	Yes	No	Yes	No	Yes
West Bengal	Yes	Yes	Yes	Yes	No	Yes	No	Yes

Source: World Bank compilation.
Note: ABT = ability-based tariff; CGRF = consumer grievance-redressal forum; MYT = multiyear tariff; SAC = state advisory committee.

Table G.4 Implementation of Mandates Data: Open Access and Renewable Energy/Energy Efficiency

State	OA regulations	OA surcharge	OA wheeling charge	OA transmission charge	Number of OA applications received	RPO regulations	Technology-specific RPOs	RPO compliance monitored	Energy efficiency and DSM regulations	FIT regulations	ToD metering regulations	Provision for ToD tariff
Andhra Pradesh	Yes	Yes	Yes	Yes	11	Yes	Yes	Yes	No	Yes	Yes	Yes
Assam	Yes	Yes	Yes	Yes	0	Yes	Yes	No	No	Yes	Yes	Yes
Bihar	Yes	Yes	Yes	Yes	0	Yes	Yes	Yes	No	Yes	Yes	Yes
Chhattisgarh	Yes	Yes	Yes	Yes	16	Yes	Yes	No	Yes	Yes	Yes	Yes
Delhi	Yes	Yes	Yes	Yes	0	Yes	Yes	No	No	Yes	Yes	Yes
Goa	Yes	No	No	No	0	Yes	Yes	Yes	No	No	No	No
Gujarat	Yes	Yes	Yes	Yes	44	Yes	Yes	Yes	No	Yes	Yes	Yes
Haryana	Yes	No	Yes	Yes	2	Yes	Yes	Yes	Yes	Yes	No	No
Himachal Pradesh	Yes	Yes	Yes	Yes	3	Yes	Yes	Yes	Yes	Yes	Yes	Yes
Other	Yes	Yes	No	Yes	0	Yes	Yes	Yes	Yes	Yes	No	No
Jharkhand	Yes	Yes	Yes	Yes	1	Yes	Yes	Yes	Yes	Yes	Yes	Yes
Karnataka	Yes	Yes	Yes	Yes	11	Yes	Yes	Yes	No	Yes	Yes	Yes
Kerala	Yes	Yes	No	Yes	1	Yes	Yes	Yes	No	Yes	Yes	Yes
Madhya Pradesh	Yes	Yes	Yes	Yes	33	Yes	Yes	Yes	No	Yes	Yes	Yes
Maharashtra	Yes	Yes	Yes	Yes	64	Yes	No	Yes	Yes	Yes	Yes	Yes
Manipur and Mizoram	Yes	No	No	No	0	Yes	Yes	Yes	Yes	Yes	Yes	No
Meghalaya	Yes	Yes	No	Yes	0	Yes	No	Yes	Yes	No	Yes	No
Orissa	Yes	Yes	Yes	Yes	1	Yes	Yes	Yes	Yes	Yes	Yes	Yes
Punjab	Yes	Yes	Yes	Yes	4	Yes	No	No	Yes	Yes	No	No
Rajasthan	Yes	Yes	Yes	Yes	33	Yes	No	Yes	No	Yes	Yes	Yes
Tamil Nadu	Yes	Yes	Yes	Yes	0	Yes	No	Yes	No	Yes	Yes	No
Tripura	Yes	No	No	No	0	Yes	No	No	Yes	No	Yes	No
Uttar Pradesh	Yes	Yes	Yes	Yes	29	Yes	Yes	No	No	Yes	No	Yes
Uttarakhand	Yes	Yes	Yes	Yes	0	Yes	Yes	Yes	No	Yes	Yes	Yes
West Bengal	Yes	Yes	Yes	Yes	4	Yes	Yes	Yes	No	Yes	Yes	Yes

Source: World Bank compilation.
Note: OA = open access; RPO = renewable purchase obligation; DSM = demand-side management; FIT = feed-in-tariff; ToD = time-of-day.

Environmental Benefits Statement

The World Bank Group is committed to reducing its environmental footprint. In support of this commitment, the Publishing and Knowledge Division leverages electronic publishing options and print-on-demand technology, which is located in regional hubs worldwide. Together, these initiatives enable print runs to be lowered and shipping distances decreased, resulting in reduced paper consumption, chemical use, greenhouse gas emissions, and waste.

The Publishing and Knowledge Division follows the recommended standards for paper use set by the Green Press Initiative. Whenever possible, books are printed on 50 percent to 100 percent postconsumer recycled paper, and at least 50 percent of the fiber in our book paper is either unbleached or bleached using Totally Chlorine Free (TCF), Processed Chlorine Free (PCF), or Enhanced Elemental Chlorine Free (EECF) processes.

More information about the Bank's environmental philosophy can be found at http://crinfo.worldbank.org/wbcrinfo/node/4.